DISCOVERING
ANGLO-SAXON
ENGLAND

DISCOVERING ANGLO-SAXON ENGLAND

Martin Welch

THE PENNSYLVANIA STATE UNIVERSITY PRESS
University Park, Pennsylvania

First published in Great Britain in 1992 by B.T. Batsford Ltd as
English Heritage Book of Anglo-Saxon England

First published in the United States of America in 1993 by The Pennsylvania
State University Press, Suite C, 820 North University Drive, University Park,
PA 16802

Library of Congress Cataloging-in-Publication Data
Welch, Martin G.
    Discovering Anglo-Saxon England / Martin Welch.
      p.   cm.
    Includes bibliographical references and index.
    ISBN 0-271-00894-6 (pbk. : acid-free paper)
    1. Great Britain–History–Anglo-Saxon period. 449-1066.
  2. England–Antiquities. 3. Anglo-Saxons. I. Title.
DA152.W43   1993
942.01–dc20   92-10898
                                                          CIP

Typeset by Lasertext Ltd, Stretford, Manchester M32 0JT
Printed in Great Britain by Butler & Tanner Ltd, Frome, Somerset

This book is printed on acid-free paper.

It is the policy of The Pennsylvania State University Press to use acid-free
paper for the first printing of all clothbound books. Publications on uncoated
stock satisfy minimum requirements of American National Standard for
Information Sciences—Permanence of Paper for Printed Library Materials,
ANSI Z239.48–1984.

Contents

Illustrations

Color plates

Acknowledgments

A significant number of the illustrations for this book were specially prepared in the English Heritage drawing office and I should particularly like to thank Peter Dunn for his magnificent new watercolor reconstructions of the Yeavering royal villa and the Sutton Hoo ship burial, as well as an illustration of the range of female regional dress fashions in the sixth century. I should also like to express my gratitude to the many colleagues and students over the years with whom I have shared discussions. They have all helped me to form my present views on Anglo-Saxon archaeology. Special thanks are due to both Chris Scull, who ran a critical eye over earlier drafts and also to my wife, Hazel Newey, for finding the time to read several draft chapters. Needless to say any remaining errors are solely the author's responsibility. Finally I should like to dedicate this book to our son Edward, whose development from baby to boy paralleled its composition.

The author and the publishers are grateful to the following for giving permission to reproduce illustrations: Ashmolean Museum **1**, **64**, **67**, **71**, **72**, **77**; RAI **5**, **6**, **7**, **8**, **32**, **33**, all drawn by Simon James; Niedersächsisches Institut für historische Küstenforschung **17**, **18**, **19**; Society of Antiquaries **20**; Cambridge University Committee for Aerial Photography **26**, **27**, **28**, **29**, **48**, **68**, **87**, **88**; David Miles and the Oxford Archaeological Unit **37**, **38**, **49**; William Filmer-Sankey and the Snape Historical Trust **39**; Chichester District Archaeological Unit **46**, **56**; Kent Archaeological Society and Mrs Hawkes **50**; Phaidon **51**, from J. Campbell (ed.) *The Anglo-Saxons*; the Landscape Archaeology Section of the Norfolk Museums Service, particularly Derek Edwards **57**, **58**, **59**; **60**; **color plates 2** and **3**; Norwich Castle Museum **69**; Salisbury and South Wiltshire Museum **63**; Sutton Hoo Research Trust **65**; Leslie Webster **66**; Trustees of the British Museum **76**; Department of Coins & Medals, British Museum **89**; Dr G. Speake **83**; RCHME **85**; Robin Daniels and Cleveland Archaeology **86**; Gustav Milne, the Museum of London **90**; Wiltshire Archaeological & Natural History Society, Devizes **color plate 4**; Canterbury Heritage Museum **color plate 6**; Southampton City Council **color plate 7**; The Bede Monastery Museum **color plate 8**.

1

Introduction

No book of this size can begin to do full justice to the entire Anglo-Saxon period which covers nearly seven centuries (*c.* AD 400-1066). Instead of attempting to provide equal coverage, I will concentrate on the first three centuries (*c.*400-700). This is the crucial period of settlement and conquest by Angles, Saxons, Jutes and other peoples from north Germany and south Scandinavia. They created England, the land of the Angles, from lowland Britain. Archaeology provides us with most of our knowledge, for this is in fact a period of protohistory. That is, the basis of our understanding falls somewhere between the total reliance placed on archaeology for prehistory and the primary importance of contemporary written sources in a full historical period.

The written sources

Historians view the true history of England as beginning with the seventh century. It is inextricably linked to the introduction of Latin literacy by the Christian Church of Rome. The Anglo-Saxons brought with them to Britain a runic alphabet, for short inscriptions occasionally survive on some of their metalwork and pots. Yet there is no evidence that they ever attempted to record the oral traditions of their earlier history in writing prior to the arrival of the Roman mission in 597.

The Venerable Bede was the first historian of the Anglo-Saxons. He was a monk in north-east England, educated in the late seventh century, acquiring a fluent command of both Latin and Greek. His scholarship was certainly remarkable, but his reputation today largely rests on his famous *Ecclesiastical History of the English Peoples*, written within the first third of the eighth century. Its main purpose was to describe the long, drawn-out process by which successive Anglo-Saxon regional kingdoms received Christian missions from both Rome and the Irish church. The process began in 597 with the kingdom of Kent and finished in the 670s and 680s with Sussex and the Isle of Wight. As Bede was highly selective over what he included and excluded, his text needs to be read with care. Still, for the seventh century it remains our most valuable source.

For his account of the first arrival of the Anglo-Saxons, Bede made use of a Latin sermon by a British monk called Gildas written early in the sixth century. This diatribe against the sinful lives of past and contemporary British rulers portrays the Saxons as God's weapon of vengeance on the British in Old Testament style. Bede did his best to make sense of its information and attempted to provide AD dates for his version. Nowadays we suspect that Gildas did not necessarily place events in either their correct sequence or time scale.

Compilations of the ninth century, such as the *British History* (popularly known as Nennius) and the *Anglo-Saxon Chronicle* present further problems of interpretation to the historian. For example, the *Chronicle* was a product of the West Saxon royal court and is concerned with glorifying the royal ancestry of Alfred the Great. Manipulation of royal genealogies, in this and other sources, to enhance the claims of present rulers was common. Literary formulas associated with 'origin myths' are a feature of its earlier entries. When Aelle and his three sons land from three ships on a beach named after one of the sons, we are reading legend rather than real history. Also the chronicle format ideally provides an entry for each and every year. This required a year to be assigned

1 *Saxon bossed cremation pot with a 'standing arch' design between each boss, fifth century, from Abingdon (Oxon.).*

to each event, even when the compiler really did not know when it took place. Historians now believe that none of the dates attributed to the fifth century should be accepted at face-value and matters are little better for most of the sixth century.

The influence of churchmen on the rulers of Anglo-Saxon England from the seventh century onwards was profound. Missionaries sent from Rome and Frankish Gaul (modern-day France, Belgium and the Rhineland of the Netherlands and Germany) brought with them important concepts of administration, law codes and the issuing of coinage, derived from the practices of the Roman Empire. The survival of so many aspects of Roman organization and life in the former continental provinces of the Western Roman Empire stands in great contrast to their apparent disappearance in those parts of Roman Britain settled by the Anglo-Saxons. If we are to understand why this is so, we must establish the nature and scale of the Anglo-Saxon settlements themselves.

The Anglo-Saxon migration

This has become a matter of some controversy in recent years, as some archaeologists seem determined to believe that very few immigrants from northern Germany and southern Scandinavia were involved in the creation of Anglo-Saxon England from post-Roman Britain. They see a small number of well-armed warrior bands successfully mounting a series of *coups d'état*, taking over British regional 'kingdoms'. It is further assumed that for the most part these warriors married native British women and that they and their mixed-blood 'Anglo-Saxon' progeny are the occupants of the many so-called Anglo-Saxon burial grounds studied by archaeologists.

There are real problems in accepting such a viewpoint. Firstly it argues that we know much better than both contemporary and slightly later commentators who wrote about events in Britain. It is not particularly clear what the compiler of a fifth century *Gallic Chronicle* was implying when he states that Britain had come 'under the control of the Saxons'. On the other hand, when Gildas describes the settlement of Saxon mercenaries in the eastern part of the island, their reinforcement and a subsequent successful rebellion, ravaging Britain from sea to sea, this suggests more than a mere handful of military adventurers. Bede felt secure in his belief that he was not of British descent and that his people, the Northumbrians, were Angles. Nor did he expect his readers in the eighth century to question these self-evident truths. Further his list of the three principal peoples who migrated here as Angles, Saxons and Jutes is echoed in the archaeological record.

Pottery vessels, and brooches and other items of decorative metalwork found in Early Anglo-Saxon cemeteries can be matched precisely back to those regions of north Germany and south Scandinavia which were their continental homelands according to Bede. Fifth-century pots with 'standing-arch' designs or elaborately-decorated bosses (1), 'supporting-arm' brooches, equal-arm brooches and saucer brooches are the principal object types linking individuals in eastern and southern England with contemporary burials in the district between the lower reaches of the rivers Weser and Elbe. This belongs to the present German State of Lower Saxony (*Niedersachsen*) and was the ancient homeland of the Saxons.

A small district near Schleswig is still called Angeln today and there are pots with simple rectilinear decoration or with shoulder bosses from cremation cemeteries in Schleswig-Holstein and the nearby Baltic island of Fyn (or Fünen), which can again be matched to those found in eastern and southern England. There even seems to be a major gap in settlement continuity within Schleswig-Holstein during this period. Perhaps Bede may not have been exaggerating by much when he wrote of continental Anglia becoming deserted as a result of the fifth-century migration to Britain.

Cruciform brooches were a common dress fitting in the regions north of the Elbe and their presence both in eastern England and in 'Jutish' Kent reflects both Anglian settlement and the reality of a link between Jutland and Kent. Again pottery forms common to both east Kent and west Jutland have been identified. Survival of these links into the early sixth century is indicated by finds of square headed brooches with a south Scandinavian art style and gold 'bracteate' pendants exported from southern Scandinavia into several Kentish cemeteries.

To return to the idea that only a few warriors were involved and that these intermarried principally with British women, it could be argued that female dress assemblages reflect regional continental 'folk costumes' in Anglo-Saxon cemeteries and suggest the possibility that many Anglo-Saxon men in fact brought their wives and families with them across the North Sea. Certainly it seems likely that important statements about personal and family identity were being expressed in the dress fittings and therefore costume. Female fashions changed over time, but we should not confuse the ease and speed with which modern urban dress fashions are adopted and abandoned with the 'rules' governing much more static and regionalized feast-day costume in rural communities. Still, marriages are recorded between Anglo-Saxon kings and British princesses in the sixth and seventh centuries and intermarriage need not have been particularly unusual. If Anglo-Saxon men required their British wives to wear and be buried in Anglo-Saxon folk dress, this would proclaim these women to have become Anglo-Saxons. Dress fittings alone then will not allow us to determine what proportion of an 'Anglo-Saxon' community might or might not be of native British descent.

Cremation burial was widely practised throughout virtually all areas settled by the Anglo-Saxons and provides a stronger argument against a minimal Anglo-Saxon migration. While cremation had been used in the early Roman period, it was subsequently largely abandoned in Britain, as in other Roman provinces. Inhumation seems to have been the dominant form of burial by the fourth century. The introduction of new and distinctively different cremation cemetery practices to Britain by the Anglo-Saxons seems undeniable.

Charred bones of adults and children were placed in handmade pottery containers, which almost precisely match pots found in the cremation urnfields of north Germany and southern Scandinavia. Other objects, such as miniature toilet implements, sometimes accompany the cremated bone. Once again, these match those found in the continental homeland cemeteries and contrast with earlier Romano-British cremation practices. Surely this must suggest the movement of complete families and communities across the North Sea, rather than rapid adoption by the native population of burial practices introduced by a few newcomers.

Of course, even if we add up the total number of Anglo-Saxon cremation pots and inhumation graves recorded by chance discoveries or excavated by archaeologists, the estimated figures are not enormous. But then the interpretation of such figures in order to make estimates of the size of populations is hardly a straightforward matter. The known cemetery sites have rarely been fully explored and represent an unknown proportion of the original total of burial sites established or in use between the fifth and seventh centuries. It is a rash scholar who uses the number of known burials in order to minimize the scale of the Anglo-Saxon migration and settlement.

Linguistic and place-name evidence

Language history also suggests that the number of Anglo-Saxon migrants may have been considerable. The Anglo-Saxon peoples spoke a variety of Germanic dialects which are ancestral to modern English. By contrast, the native inhabitants of post-Roman Britain spoke Celtic languages ancestral to later Welsh and Cornish, though some will have possessed a more or less limited command of Latin. If only a few Anglo-Saxon immigrants actually crossed the North Sea, it is difficult to see why English became the dominant language in lowland Britain, replacing Celtic dialects there.

The study of place-names during the present century has demonstrated the thoroughness with which most of the landscape came to be renamed in Old English. Of course, this picture has to be modified for eastern and northern England by the undoubted impact of later Scandinavian settlers speaking related Germanic languages in the Viking period (ninth to eleventh centuries) on both dialects and place-names. By contrast, the imposition of a Norman military aristocracy after the Conquest of 1066 had a relatively limited affect on the place-names of England. French was even supplanted by English as the language of the royal court and the aristocracy in the fourteenth century. It may be that both the Anglo-Saxons and the Scandinavians in the Viking period settled in some numbers and as farmers working the land themselves, rather than just as landlords. This may help to explain the renaming of the landscape and the triumph of English over Celtic dialects.

Anglo-Saxon studies and archaeology

The serious study of the written heritage of the Anglo-Saxons in both Latin and Old English dates back to the seventeenth century. That century also produced the first documented account of pots from an Anglo-Saxon cremation cemetery. True, Sir Thomas Browne mistook the urns from Norfolk for Roman burials and it never occurred to him that they might belong to his Anglo-Saxon forbears. Study of classical literature encouraged such thoughts, and Bryan Faussett similarly believed that the inhumation burials he excavated in Kent between 1759 and 1773 belonged to 'Romans Britonized' and 'Britons Romanized'. Much of his fine collection of objects is now in Liverpool Museum together with his excellent notebooks which record each grave in considerable detail.

It was James Douglas who first realized that Faussett's cemeteries and a number which he himself excavated belonged to Anglo-Saxons.

His publication of *Nenia Britannica* in 1793 marks the real beginning of Anglo-Saxon archaeology. The nineteenth century saw further developments linked to a greater public awareness of the destruction of the archaeological heritage which accompanied the expansion of towns and the construction of railways. The publication of Faussett's notebooks, edited by Charles Roach Smith in 1856 under the title of *Inventorium Sepulchrale* was a major achievement. So was J.M. Kemble's article published in 1855, which showed that cremation pots excavated near Stade by the Elbe matched urns recovered from Anglo-Saxon cemeteries in England.

A number of important excavations of Anglo-Saxon cemeteries were mounted in the second half of the nineteenth century, for instance W.M. Wylie at Fairford (Gloucestershire) in 1850-51, J.Y. Akerman at Brighthampton in 1857 and Long Wittenham in 1859-60, both near Oxford, and G.W. Thomas at Sleaford (Lincolnshire) in 1882. Syntheses which attempted to bring all this evidence together and place it in its historical context appeared in the years before and during the First World War. E.T. Leeds of the Ashmolean Museum in Oxford produced his first survey of Anglo-Saxon archaeology in 1913 and volumes III and IV of *The Arts in Early England* were published by G. Baldwin Brown, Professor of Art at Edinburgh University in 1915.

Another major landmark was provided by the 1939 discovery of the rich unrobbed ship burial at Sutton Hoo. The work that went into the conservation and restoration of this find for display in the British Museum stimulated great interest after the Second World War. Television programmes were made to explain this major find to the public and both the re-investigation of the ship burial in the 1960s and the recent campaign to excavate a representative sample of the Sutton Hoo cemetery have attracted media interest.

Anglo-Saxon cemetery studies have benefited from the postwar expansion and increasing professionalism of archaeology, which has provided us with a wealth of new data from modern controlled excavations. Several major cemetery reports have been published in the last decade or are due to appear in print shortly, with financial and academic support from English Heritage. Efforts to achieve complete excavations of extensive burial grounds as at Mucking (cemetery II) in Essex and Spong Hill in Norfolk between the late 1960s and the 1980s have provided us with much larger samples, which can be analysed by statistical methods. All this has enabled us to ask new questions of the archaeological evidence from cemeteries which will be considered in Chapter 6.

Archaeological excavation of the settlements associated with these cemeteries had to wait until the 1920s and the pioneer efforts by E.T. Leeds to investigate a 'village' near Sutton Courtenay, Oxfordshire. Even then the excavation techniques applied were not adequate by modern standards. It was the relatively late adoption of excavation methods first developed in the Netherlands, north Germany and Denmark in the 1920s and 1930s, which enabled British archaeologists to begin to recover the shadowy traces of timber buildings from the 1950s onwards. B. Hope-Taylor led the way with his meticulous excavation at Yeavering in Northumberland. This and more recent excavations have revolutionized our understanding of Early Anglo-Saxon settlements, the 'communities in life' of the next three chapters.

2

Buildings and settlement organization

When visiting an Early Anglo-Saxon settlement site there is usually nothing on the ground surface to show that it was there. By contrast, building platforms and trackways of a later medieval village can show as clearly visible bumps and hollows in a field, which can be photographed from the air and mapped. It is not until the ploughsoil is removed that the foundations of the timber buildings in which Anglo-Saxons ate, slept and worked can be picked out. Until the end of the 1960s, relatively little was known about Anglo-Saxon rural settlements of the fifth to seventh centuries or indeed later. It is only recently that we could claim to know the full range of buildings used as houses, stores and workshops, or the organization and layout of settlements. English archaeologists lagged behind their colleagues in northern Europe, whose successful excavation of sites occupied by the ancestors of the Anglo-Saxon migrants, from the 1920s onwards, showed what could be achieved. The need to find and systematically excavate Early Anglo-Saxon rural settlements became a priority in the 1960s and 1970s and was to pay handsome dividends (2).

Chalton

Sites located on the chalk downlands of southern England produce particularly clear results. Once the topsoil has been removed, the dark soil fills of the post-holes and trenches left by rectangular timber buildings and fenced enclosures stand out clearly against the soft white bedrock of chalk. One settlement on Church Down in the parish of Chalton (Hampshire) was systematically excavated over six seasons between 1970 and 1976. The aim was to recover the plan of every building and

reconstruct the layout of the settlement. This occupied the southern end of a long ridge, which overlooks the coastal plain of south-east Hampshire and beyond, across the Solent, the Isle of Wight can be clearly seen. Unusually it had been identified as a result of a programme of fieldwalking made possible by the keen co-operation of the local farmer. He could remember ploughing this field as a young man shortly after the Second World War and seeing rectangular patches of dark soil emerging which contained occupation debris from the floor levels of Anglo-Saxon buildings, though he did not realize this at the time.

In the late 1960s the ploughsoil still contained quite a few recognizable fragments of Early Anglo-Saxon pottery, parts of fired clay loomweights and animal bone fragments. There was sufficient material to indicate a probability that the remains of a settlement existed below the topsoil. In practice it is rare for an Early Anglo-Saxon site to be discovered in this way, because the pottery of the period was poorly made and has a tendency to disintegrate in ploughsoil. Vessels were handmade, without the use of a turntable or potter's wheel, by coiling clay and then smoothing it out. Pots were fired at fairly low temperatures in little more than covered bonfires called clamp-kilns.

Trial excavation in 1970 revealed the relatively well-preserved foundations for timber buildings and fence lines dug into the chalk bedrock. The method of excavation involved the clearance of areas large enough to include the complete plans of several timber buildings at a time, which is why it is referred to as open

2 *Map of principal sites discussed in chapters 2–4.*

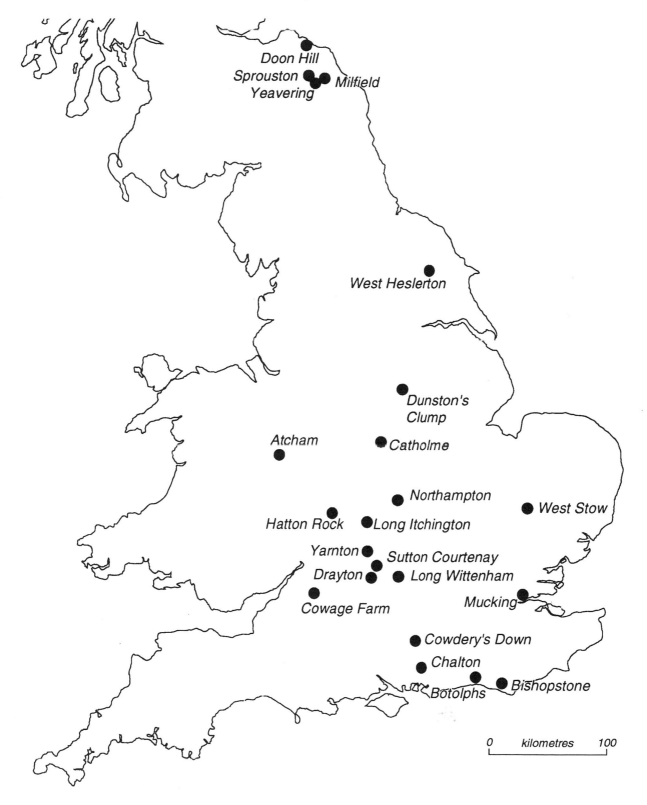

0   150   Ft

0   50 M

3 *Plan showing all the excavated structures on Church Down, Chalton (Hants.). There were four successive sets of buildings organized into farm units, like those found complete in the north-east corner of this seventh-century settlement.*

area excavation (**3**). The first 15cm (6in) or so of topsoil was removed either by hand with pickaxe and shovels or by machine for greater speed. Then the upper surface of the chalk was cleared using garden forks to loosen the compacted soil, shovels removed it and thick-bristled brushes gave a final clean off. It then became easy to see the patches and lines of dark soil, which reveal where man-made holes had been dug into the white bedrock.

Lines of small circular patches or post-holes were visible; these were pits for individual timbers which provided the basic framework for rectangular buildings. Other structures with similar rectangular plans had their earthfast timber uprights spaced along narrow trenches dug through the soil into the bedrock. In one zone where buildings from different stages in the development of the settlement overlapped, it emerged that the trench-foundation represented a later type of construction method replacing the individual post-hole type. Zig-zag patterns of small individual post-holes set in lines seemed to represent offset timber uprights, which clasped horizontal planking to form low wooden fences.

Of the 61 buildings revealed in the excavations, 57 had rectangular plans. Based on earthfast timber uprights, their floors were either of beaten earth or suspended timber planking above ground level. Archaeologists usually describe them as 'halls', but if by this word is meant a place where people eat, drink and maybe also sleep, then probably only a proportion of the ground-level rectangular buildings at Chalton really deserve the term. There was a considerable variety of size among the Chalton 'halls'. The larger ones such as A1 and A2 measured around 11m long by 6.3m wide (36 by 20ft), whereas the middle range of buildings were typically 8.5m by 5.3m (28ft by 17ft).

Both the larger and medium-sized structures shared a similar plan, based on a double square separated in the middle by the width of two doorways, placed opposite one another at the centre of each long wall. Almost all the larger halls possessed an internal wooden partition separating off one end of the building, taking in an area of about one fifth of the total. Occasionally a patch of less-worn chalk within the main area of the hall was found, which might record the position of a hearth for both cooking and heating the building.

The smallest buildings had only one doorway, again in the middle of one of the long sides. A version of these small halls is provided by a sequence of at least four structures, one built next to the site of another, within the south-west quadrant of the settlement. These did not necessarily all exist at the same time, but might have been successively built and demolished, one after the other. They shared the unusual feature of a row of internal post-holes placed

down the central axis of each building, about which more will be said in the next chapter.

It is only in the north-east quadrant of the site that there was sufficient overlap between buildings to demonstrate that the settlement went through at least four phases of construction and reconstruction. Preservation there of complete fence-line enclosures as well as hall plans allow us to see three complete settlement units. Each consisted of a large hall set east-west with a fenced square or rectangular enclosure attached to its east gable wall. Each enclosure contained two or three smaller halls. It seems reasonable to interpret these units as individual farms, each belonging to a single family. They would have lived, eaten and slept in the large hall and presumably used the buildings inside the fence enclosures for storage and as workshops. Despite modern plough damage, shorter sections of fence lines were preserved elsewhere within the settlement, implying that most of the excavated rectangular hall buildings at Chalton were components of similar farm units.

Cowdery's Down

This pattern of farm and fenced yard was found again at a settlement discovered at the very end of the 1970s on Cowdery's Down near Basingstoke (Hampshire) (4). The excavation of a large rectangular ditched enclosure unexpectedly revealed past Anglo-Saxon occupation. The enclosure had shown up as a cropmark on air photographs and turned out to be of Iron Age date. Absolutely no indication of the Anglo-Saxon buildings and fence-lines had been revealed by the air views, but they showed up extremely clearly against the white chalk once the topsoil had been scraped off the bedrock. As a modern housing estate was going to be built there, the opportunity was taken to explore the Anglo-Saxon settlement as fully as possible in 1980 and 1981.

Three successive phases of timber building construction were preserved. Building A1 had a plan based on post-holes aligned east-west and attached to it was the western fence-line of a double farm enclosure, which contained structure A3 in its southern enclosure and A2 in the northern one. Hall B4 replaced Hall A1 and had post-holes set east-west and inserted through the same western fence-line immediately north of A1. The southern enclosure now contained a small shed B5 and the northern

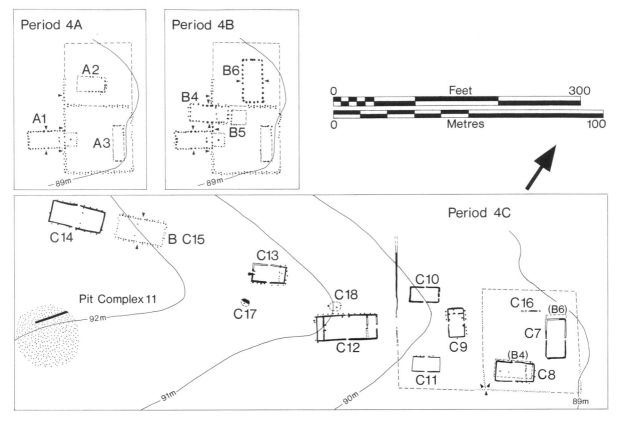

4 *Plan showing the three successive building phases on Cowdery's Down (Hants.). The first two phases consist of a pair of fenced farm units with plank-in-posthole buildings (periods 4A and 4B). These are rebuilt on the same site in a new layout of two farm units with plank-in-trench buildings in period 4C, together with a series of much larger halls to the west and two sunken featured buildings.*

enclosure had building B6. All these halls and their paired enclosures were then removed and a completely new pair of fenced enclosures was constructed (fence C) containing six rectangular buildings based on uprights set in narrow trenches. Once again halls with trench-constructed foundations replace structures with individual post-hole foundations. To the south-west of the fenced enclosures several more timber buildings attributed to this third phase were excavated, including a series of extremely large halls, which will be discussed further in Chapter 4. Phase C ended abruptly when all its buildings were destroyed by fire. Whether this was a result of an accident, an

act of war, or simply the most effective way for its inhabitants to demolish a settlement they were leaving, is something we will never know.

By chance a hedge, which could be dated back as far as the seventeenth century, had helped to preserve details of the timber construction in the post-holes and trenches here. These had not been detected at Chalton. Soil stains, the result of finer soil particles replacing the rotting and carbonized timbers, demonstrate that oak planks were used as the principal earthfast uprights both in individual 'post-holes' and in wall trench foundations (5 and 6). The planks had been narrower at one edge than the other, because they had been radially split from the trunk using axes and wedges, and were not sawn. These planks were fastened together using wooden pegs (trenails) and joints to create a wall framework. This was then infilled with wattle panels made from interwoven thin branches and windproofed by being daubed with clay. It is quite possible that these wattle-and-daub panels were white-washed or painted and some of the timbers may well have been decorated with chiselled and

18

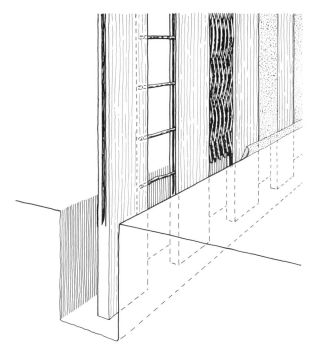

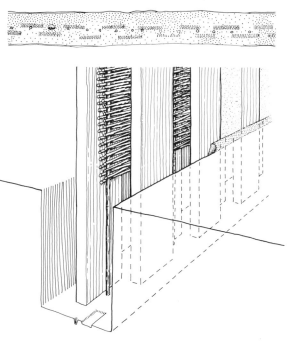

5 *Reconstruction of the timber wall based on impressions of evenly-spaced vertical planks in the trenches of Cowdery's Down Hall C9. The gaps were probably filled with panels of interwoven branches or wattles daubed with clay to make it weatherproof.*

6 *Reconstruction of the timber wall based on two staggered lines of evenly-spaced plank impressions and between them a row of stake-holes to take a wattled frame in the trenches of Cowdery's Down Hall C12. The wattling filled the space between the planks and was daubed with clay for weatherproofing*

carved ornament and the details picked out with paint. Certainly there is absolutely no need to assume that these buildings looked dull.

The information obtained from the exercise of turning the Cowdery's Down evidence into viable building reconstructions, in the form of three-dimensional drawings (**7**), led the team there to suggest a series of reconstructions for the Chalton buildings. These are radically different from those first proposed by Chalton's own excavators. For example, a row of post-holes outside and parallel to the outer wall represent neither uprights for a verandah, nor true buttresses. Rather they would have held planks angled in to support the horizontal planks running along the top of the wall. These horizontal planks are referred to as wall plates and it seems probable that the angled plank supports helped to counter any torsion motion in the wall plate caused by the downforce of the weight of the roof which would tend to push the walls outwards. Careful measurement of the angles of the timbers at Cowdery's Down

implies that the wall plates there were set surprisingly low, well below head height.

It follows that if the occupants or users of these buildings were not to spend much of their time indoors bent double, the door frames must have extended up well above wall plate level into the roof area and that the roof will probably have been supported on substantial curved timber frames called crucks. Together these would have provided sufficient headroom for people to stand upright in any part of the building. The material used to roof these buildings might have been thatch or thin tiles of timber known as shingles. At present there is no way of deciding which was used, but a different angle would have been required for each, so that an effective run-off for rainwater was provided.

Interestingly in the case of the farm unit based on Hall AZ1 at Chalton, there was a doorway at the east end of the building, and it would have been possible to walk directly from the hall into the enclosure. This was certainly

19

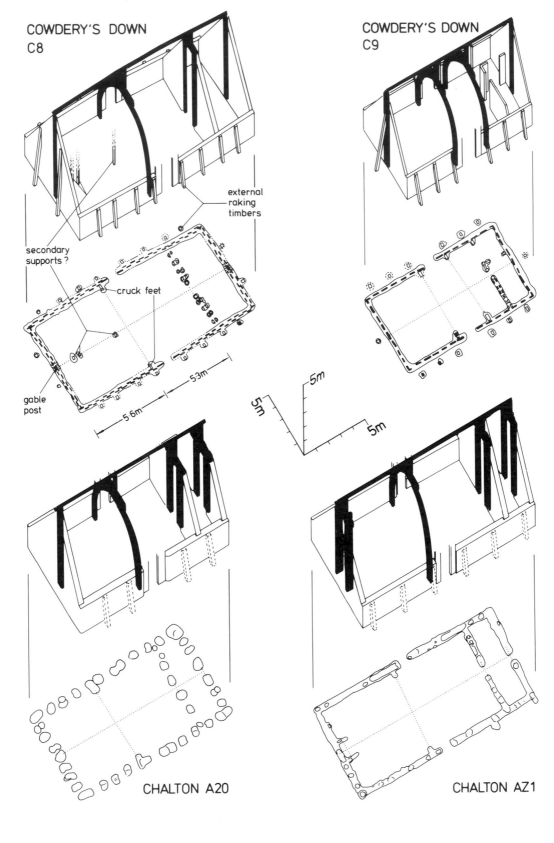

COWDERY'S DOWN
C8

COWDERY'S DOWN
C9

external
raking
timbers

secondary
supports ?

cruck feet

5·3m

5m

5m

5m

gable
post

5·6m

CHALTON A20

CHALTON AZ1

not the case for halls A1 and B4 at Cowdery's Down where it would have been necessary to walk out through one of the main doors in the long side and then pass through a narrow entrance between the building and the fence (**8**). So narrow were these fence entrances at Cowdery's Down that it seems highly improbable that large livestock such as cattle or sheep were ever herded into them. Of course, domestic fowl such as geese or chickens would pose no problems, but it may be that the fences were there to protect herb gardens and vegetable plots growing within the enclosure from grazing animals.

Just four of the buildings at Chalton belong to a completely different building type based on a hollowed-out rectangular pit with rounded corners dug into the chalk bedrock. The roof which covered this hollow would have rested on a horizontal timber, or ridge pole, which ran between two post uprights. Each earthfast upright was based in a post-hole at either end of the hollow, though in one case at Chalton, the post-holes were located outside an unusually small pit. The standard term for this building type is a German word: *Grubenhaus*, meaning a 'pit house' (plural form: *Grubenhäuser*) and English archaeologists used to call them 'sunken huts'. More recently the rather long-winded 'sunken featured building', or SFB for short, has become the standard term. This, it is argued, has the advantage of making no preconceived judgements as to whether the base of the hollow pit formed the floor of the building, or whether there was a suspended wooden floor at a higher level.

7 *Reconstructions of Cowdery's Down Halls C8 and C9 together with Chalton Halls A20 and AZ1. The low height of the walls is estimated from the angled external timbers, which braced the wall plate. The outer door frames extend into the roof and internal support for the roof timbers is provided by one or two pairs of curved timbers (crucks) set next to the door frames. The internal posts in Hall C8 are later repairs and not part of the original structure.*

West Stow

At a settlement on a low sandy knoll in the valley of the river Lark near West Stow (Suffolk), we can examine the evidence for *Grubenhäuser* as examples have been reconstructed with raised suspended wooden floors over hollows used as cellars. As at Chalton, the aim of the West Stow project (1965-72) was to excavate the site systematically in large open areas and provide a reasonably complete plan of Anglo-Saxon occupation. Some buildings had already been partially or completely destroyed in the north-east corner and a strip running north-south across the middle of the site was left unexcavated because of trees along a hedgeline. Also, the southern edge of the excavation is so close to any number of buildings belonging to the settlement that we may presume that several more structures await investigation here. Nevertheless the greater part of the settlement has been excavated, recorded and now published while the full report on Chalton is yet to appear.

The West Stow buildings recognizably belong to the same forms as those found at Chalton. There are both rectangular post-built halls and a wide variety of *Grubenhäuser*. It is the proportion of halls to sunken featured buildings which distinguishes West Stow from Chalton. There were many more *Grubenhäuser*, 69 in all, but only seven halls, together with a further seven or more smaller rectangular post-built structures. Chalton had just four *Grubenhäuser* to 59 rectangular buildings. Also there were no recognizable fence lines at West Stow, though there were a series of ditches which seem to function as boundary markers in the last phase of Anglo-Saxon occupation there.

Two of the West Stow *Grubenhäuser* (SFB 3 and 15) had been destroyed by fire and this had preserved carbonized timber planking within the hollow pit (**9**). Some of the planks underlay clay loomweights and were interpreted reasonably enough as floorboards, on which an upright weaving loom had stood at the time of the fire. Other planking lay over the loomweights and was seen as belonging to side walls, which had collapsed inwards. In addition, a fine silty sand was detected at the very base of the hollow. This was interpreted as the result of fine-grained material seeping through very narrow gaps between the floorboards.

The controversial part of the excavator's interpretation concerns the level at which the

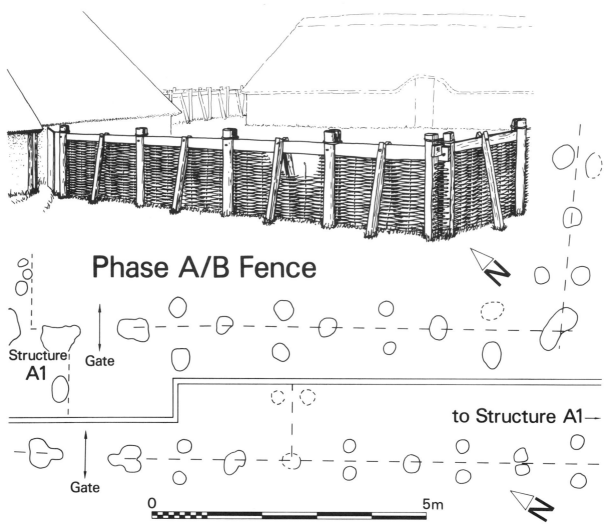

Phase A/B Fence

Structure A1

Gate

to Structure A1→

Gate

0   5m

8 *Reconstruction of the low fence adjacent to Cowdery's Down Hall A1 based on pairs of timbers clasping long planks at the top of the fence, further supported by pairs of angled timbers. A narrow entrance (probably a gate) between hall and fence was wide enough for humans but far too narrow for cattle and sheep.*

planked floor was constructed. He believes that it was set just above the natural ground level, with the greater part of the floor suspended over the hollow pit, which then becomes a shallow cellar. It is proposed that a rectangular frame of squared timbers may have been laid directly on the ground surface around the hollow (**10**). This would leave little or no trace for the archaeologist to pick up, even if the Anglo-Saxon ground surface had been preserved. Then several rafters could be jointed into this frame and the floor planks attached to the frame and rafters. The roof would be constructed on a framework based on a ridge-pole supported at either end of the hollow by upright earthfast posts. There is at least one such post at each end, but quite a few of the West Stow sunken featured buildings had three posts at each end, providing additional support to a pitched roof running the length of the structure. Finally, the side walls would have been built up from the base frame to a horizontal wall plate at the junction with the roof.

It has been suggested that one advantage of having so much of the plank floor suspended over the hollow pit is that it would take much

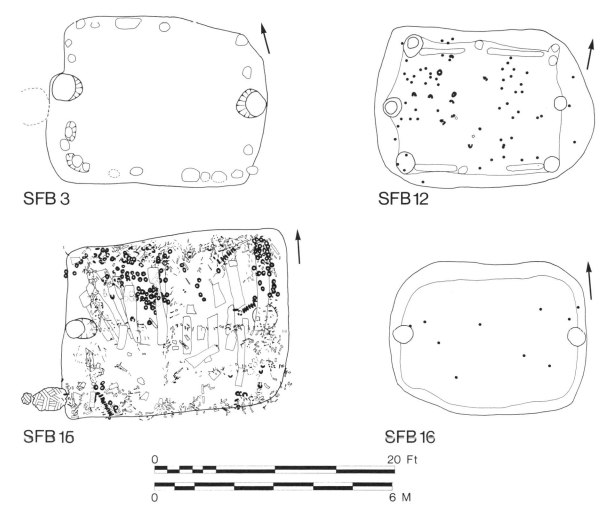

SFB 3

SFB 12

SFB 16

SFB 16

0   20 Ft

0   6 M

longer before the floorboards started to rot than would be the case with a hall. But this ignores the fact that the timber frame laid on the ground would rot first, as would the earthfast posts supporting the roof structure, and the wet-rot would spread to the floorboards eventually, making them unsafe to walk over. Still there were two further pieces of excavated evidence which were seen as supporting the concept of a suspended floor positioned above ground level.

Firstly there were several cases where a clay hearth lay partly slumped into the hollow, for instance in SFB's 44 and 49. This is interpreted as the result of constructing a clay hearth on the plank floor and its subsequent partial collapse when the rotting boards gave way. However, placing hearths close to the side

9 *Plans of* Grubenhäuser *at West Stow. SFB15 had burnt down, preserving carbonized planks above and below ring-shaped loomweights; the planks below were floor timbers and those above side walls. Post-holes and slots around the edges of SFB3, SFB12 and SFB16 suggest timbers were used to line the soft sandy pit. The small feature at the SW corner of SFB15 is part of a clay hearth sited dangerously near its side walls. Perhaps it was constructed after SFB15 had burnt down and over the backfilled pit.*

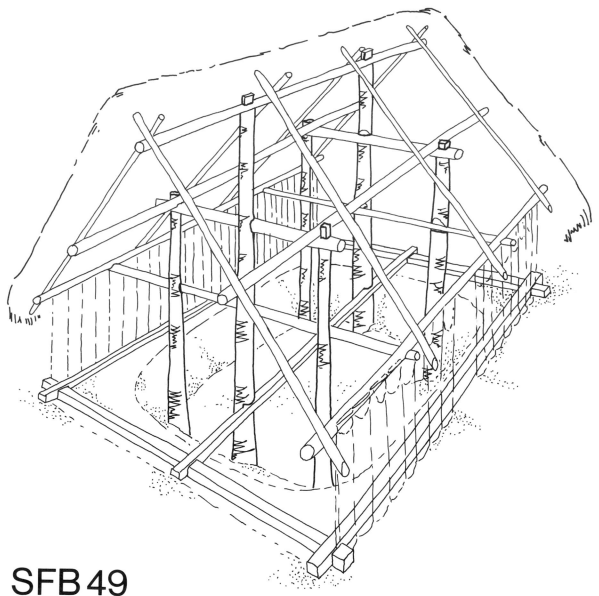

SFB 49

10 *Reconstruction of West Stow SFB49 based on six posts to support the roof and a hypothetical rectangular timber frame resting directly on the ground outside the pit, to which upright planks are attached for the side walls. Bracing timbers are placed across this rectangular frame over the pit so that floorboards can be attached.*

walls of a timber building is a rather risky procedure. The adjacent wall timbers could be covered with clay, but the danger of setting the building alight remains very real and it is more normal to place an open hearth near the centre of a timber building. Of course, this might explain why several sunken featured buildings at West Stow came to end in a blaze, but the inhabitants might be expected to have learnt this lesson fairly quickly.

Alternatively these hearths, which partly overlie both the fine silty layer at the base of the pits and the outer edge of the hollows, might follow the use of these hollows as parts of buildings. Are we therefore seeing a reuse of abandoned building pits? These would provide ready-made sheltered areas for industrial open-air hearths, used for a variety of craftwork purposes.

There are also problems in believing that the skeletons of two dogs in SFB 16 represent domestic pets or farm dogs which crawled under the floorboards into the 'cellar' to die peacefully. It is argued that their corpses decayed without being disturbed and the skulls just rolled a short distance as the bones became disarticulated. This would imply that people were actually living or working above a rotting stench and did nothing about it, which seems rather unlikely. The alternative is that the corpses of recently deceased dogs were disposed of in former building hollows, now used as rubbish pits and were at least partially covered by soil; this interpretation surely has a more believable ring to it.

The excavator compared the burnt timber evidence from the West Stow Grubenhäuser with his own personal experience, having witnessed native huts burning in Kenya. Certainly there is little reason to doubt that timber planking occurred in these buildings. It is possible to judge his reconstructions by visiting the open air museum which has been developed on the West Stow site to the north-west of Bury St Edmunds. Here there are full-size timber reconstructions of several sunken featured buildings and one of the halls. The raised timber floors over the 'cellar' hollows have a distinctly bouncy feel, caused by inadequate support from the rafters. The often substantial gaps between the floorboards make it possible to observe the rather limited capacity of the 'cellars' for storage.

One Grubenhaus has been constructed deliberately without a timber floor as an experiment to test the effect of erosion by visitors' feet on the soft sandy subsoil of the hollow. What should emerge from this experiment is the real need to line these hollow pits with timber revetment and give the base a plank floor lining. Surely the plank floor should be at the base of the hollow and the 'side walls' be the revetment lining of the pit sides (**11**). Two West Stow building plans provide evidence for postholes (SFB 3) or narrow trenches and postholes (SFB 12) around the lower edge of the hollows (see **9**). These would certainly fit this alternative type of reconstruction. Also, as the excavator of West Stow is aware, timber plank and wattle-lined Grubenhäuser are known from the continental settlement of Wijster (Netherlands), another site constructed on a sand subsoil.

If the need for a timber lining is accepted when hollows are dug into sand or soft gravel, then we have an explanation for the difficulty experienced by many excavators in identifying entrances to these Grubenhäuser. In most cases the natural ground surface which existed at the time these hollows were dug has since been eroded away by ploughing and other activities. Even if this is not so, the pitched roof over the timber-lined hollows may have come down to ground level, or rested just above it on a low earth bank or turf wall. If a wooden ladder or steep steps were used to provide access at one of the gable ends, we could not hope to detect this entrance.

Of course, if the base of a timber-lined pit represented the floor area, the overall size of these structures would be quite small. But then there is no particular reason to believe that Grubenhäuser were houses people lived in. Rather they may have been no more than basic shelters, used for craftwork such as weaving and perhaps also for general storage.

When sunken buildings were dug into a harder subsoil, such as chalk as at Chalton, there was no need to provide a timber revetment or floor. In chalkland settlements, the presence of shallow stake-holes and an accumulation of settlement debris often provide strong grounds for believing that the base of the excavated hollow served as the floor of the roofed building constructed over it. The same seems to be true of many Grubenhäuser dug into harder gravel, as at Mucking (Essex), a site which was being investigated at much the same time as the West Stow settlement.

Farm units at West Stow

If we are looking for buildings at West Stow to function as dwellings or farmhouses, we should turn our attention to the seven halls there (**12** and **13**). Their positioning is particularly significant, for each hall is isolated from the next one and each is more or less surrounded by a small cluster of sunken featured buildings. Examination of the metal finds, bone combs, pottery fragments and other debris from the fills of the sunken hollows demonstrates that

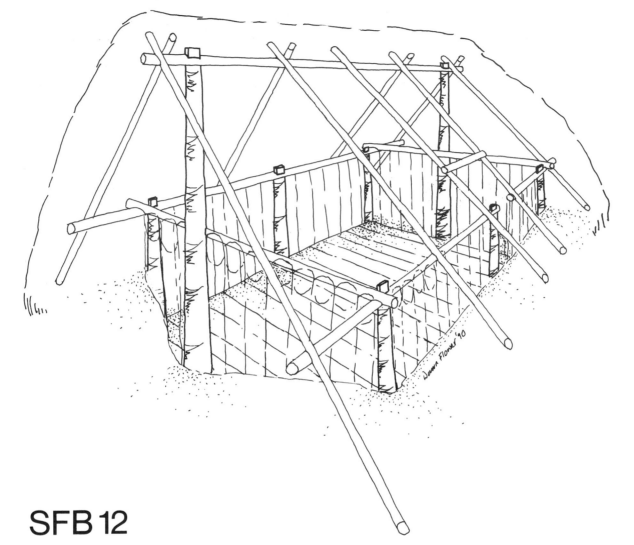

SFB 12

11 *Reconstruction of West Stow SFB12 based on six posts to support the roof. The pit is completely lined with timber planking. Access is assumed to be through one of the open gable ends using a ladder or set of steps, which would leave no trace for the archaeologist.*

these clusters of *Grubenhäuser* often seem to represent groups of contemporary buildings. It is probable that many of the finds in these hollows represent rubbish dumped into them after they ceased to be used as roofed buildings; but this still does not alter the fact that these sunken featured buildings probably represent broadly contemporary structures. Their reuse as rubbish pits will have followed on within a very short time from their abandon-

ment as buildings. Likewise most, if not all, the rubbish dumped in them is likely to have come from the immediate vicinity of these structures.

It seems reasonable to suggest that each cluster of sunken featured buildings was associated with the hall in its midst. Unfortunately as the floor levels of these halls do not survive, it has to be a working assumption that the halls really do belong with the *Grubenhäuser*. Certainly no securely stratified finds have been found in any of the halls. Heat-staining of the subsoil below a hearth was noted in more than one hall at West Stow, however, so it seems likely that families lived, cooked, ate and slept in the seven halls. In all probability the West Stow halls functioned as single family farmhouses in the same way as the halls attached to

12 *Reconstruction of West Stow Hall 2 in the open-air museum on the site of the excavated settlement near Bury St Edmunds (Suffolk).*

13 *Alternative reconstruction of West Stow Hall 2 using evidence from Cowdery's Down, with low side walls and a pair of crucks to support the roof structure behind the door frames. An area partitioned off to one side may represent a more private part of the house.*

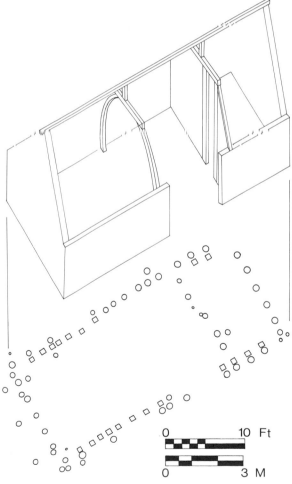

the fenced enclosures at Chalton and Cowdery's Down. Presumably the sunken featured buildings provided for a similar range of ancillary functions such as stores and workshops, which at Chalton and Cowdery's Down were largely covered by the medium- and smaller-sized rectangular buildings within the enclosures, together with a much small number of sunken featured buildings (four at Chalton and just two at Cowdery's Down).

So why are there so many sunken featured buildings at West Stow as well as at virtually every contemporary settlement built on a site with sand or gravel subsoil? Then again, why are there so few of these buildings at Chalton, Cowdery's Down and most other settlements located on chalk downland? The answer would appear to be very mundane. It is relatively easy to dig a substantial hole into sand or gravel and save on building materials by having a lowered floor covered by a pitched roof. On the other hand, it is rather harder to dig out even a soft rock like chalk. As a result, in the downland they constructed most of their ancillary buildings with earthfast planks in rectangular settings.

On occasion, even chalkland settlers felt the need to construct a few sunken featured buildings. The frequency with which clay loomweights, spindlewhorls and other items associated with textile production are found in *Grubenhaus* hollows suggests that weaving was one of the more important activities practised in them. They were to be found in the largest of the four sunken featured buildings at Chalton, which has been interpreted as a weaving hut. A damp atmosphere makes weaving easier, particularly when producing linen from flax and a covered man-made hollow would certainly fulfil this requirement.

West Heslerton

The contrast between chalkland and gravel-based settlements makes the current large-scale excavation directed by Dominic Powlesland and funded by English Heritage at West Heslerton (North Yorkshire) particularly interesting. This settlement is on the southern edge of the Vale of Pickering, partly over the lower chalk slopes of the Yorkshire Wolds and the rest over alluvial gravels. The greater part of an adjacent contemporary cemetery dating around the sixth century has been excavated to the north. So far some 150 buildings have been recorded here including both halls and *Grubenhäuser*. Soil stains indicating the presence of planking have been observed in some of the hall post-holes, and charcoal may permit the identification of the timber used. The first impression seems to be that we have here the characteristics of both settlement forms, which is appropriate since both subsoils are present.

3

Settlement dating and the rural economy

Dating an Early Anglo-Saxon settlement site is not necessarily easy. In the case of chalkland sites, the rarity of *Grubenhäuser* or other man-made pits used to dump domestic rubbish is combined with the normal plough destruction of occupation floor levels from the post-hole- or trench-constructed buildings. Even if sherds of pottery or metalwork fragments are found in a post-hole or construction trench, we cannot be sure when or how they got there. They might conceivably relate to the digging of the hole (trench), or the insertion of packed timber uprights, or to the demolition and removal of sound earthfast timbers for reuse elsewhere. We also have to consider how long this item might have been floating in the ploughsoil as residual material from earlier occupation and farming activity in the vicinity, before it came to be accidentally dumped in either a post or trench fill.

Dating Cowdery's Down

The problems are particularly acute in the case of Cowdery's Down, where even the two sunken featured buildings produced virtually no finds. There was a little Anglo-Saxon pottery from the site, but it was very unimpressive. So much so, that if the buildings of the associated settlement had not been recognized as Anglo-Saxon, most of it would have been described as fragments of post-medieval brick! Instead scientific dating methods had to be used to attempt to place in time the three successive phases over which a pair of family farm units were occupied. Two samples from structure A2 give a calibrated radiocarbon date of AD 580 ± 67 and three samples from C9 combined with two from the massive Hall C12 come out at AD 609 ± 57. A thermoluminescence date

from burnt daub in Hall C12 of AD 720 ± 147 tells us about the destruction rather than the construction of that building. Taken together they suggest an overall seventh-century date range for the settlement.

If the three phases of construction can be related to three successive human generations, then the entire lifespan of this settlement might be more or less contained within a century. The calculation of the length of a human generation derived from contemporary Anglo-Saxon cemeteries is open to criticism, however, as will be explained in more detail in Chapter 5. Our ability to diagnose correctly the age at death of those who survived their early twenties has been called into question recently. Figures of 30 to 35 years have been offered in the past for the average human lifespan in this period and will be applied here for lack of anything more reliable.

It may be that a rectangular hall based on earthfast oak planks would be a viable structure over a similar timespan. A maximum of a 40- to 50-year 'life' seems probable, but again there has not really been enough experimental work to be sure. We need to build full-size structures with freshly felled oak set into both chalkland and gravel subsoils to see how long they take to rot and become unstable. Modern softwood garden sheds and fences decay very rapidly, but we would expect oak to last longer. Unfortunately oak is very expensive today and the excavators of Cowdery's Down soon concluded that to use it in the reconstruction of one of their halls was far beyond any funds they could hope to raise. It would seem to make sense, however, if the main hall farmhouse was rebuilt once every generation, when one of the sons inherited from his father the position as head of the family. A sunken featured building might be replaced more often and it has been suggested that these had a useful 'life' of roughly half that of a hall.

Chalton

On this basis the four building phases at Chalton might represent up to 120-140 years of occupation. If the total of 61 buildings there is divided by four that gives just 15 to 16 per phase and implies an average of no more than three to four fenced farm units. This certainly cannot be described as a 'village' and perhaps hamlet would be a more appropriate label. Dating evidence is provided primarily by finds from the largest of the four sunken featured buildings and the contents of a few small rubbish pits. These imply a date range centred in the seventh century, though possibly extending back into the late sixth or on into the early eighth century. The decorated disc from a bronze hanging bowl, a chain-link, various pins and domestic knives are characteristic finds of the seventh century. A few sherds of wheelthrown pottery from northern France could be explained in terms of the farmers at Chalton supplying surplus food to an international trading settlement at Southampton called *Hamwic* (see Chapter 9). This seems more probable than the Chalton community becoming directly involved in cross-Channel trade. As *Hamwic* was not founded before the end of the seventh century and flourished until the ninth century, this pottery suggests that the occupation of Chalton continued into the early eighth century.

The date of West Stow

The date range for the West Stow settlement begins considerably earlier, within the fifth century, and abandonment took place there during the seventh century (**14**). Unfortunately the excavator exaggerated the date of foundation, claiming that it occurred within the first half of the fifth century. On the basis of the datable metal finds and pottery, however, there is no particular reason to believe that it was any earlier than the middle decades of that century. That it continued up at least until the middle of the seventh century is demonstrated by the presence of an early type of pottery shaped on a turntable (rather than turned on a powered wheel) and fired in a proper kiln, known as Ipswich Ware. Such kilns have been

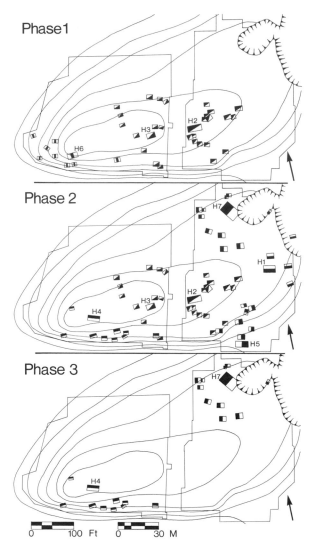

14 *Plans of West Stow in the fifth century (Phase 1), the sixth century (Phase 2) and the first half of the seventh century (Phase 3) based on pottery and other finds from the* Grubenhäuser *which form clusters around each of the seven halls. Each hall-based cluster probably represents a farm unit.*

excavated in Ipswich and production appears to have begun around the middle decades of the seventh century. So the site at West Stow seems to have been occupied over some two hundred years or a little less, that is perhaps six generations. Another settlement which may well be its successor has been identified from scatters of Ipswich Ware in the topsoil further upstream, about a mile to the south-east, but this site has yet to be excavated.

Once again, West Stow was certainly not a village, although it is described as such on the title page of the published report. Rather it was a small hamlet which never contained more than four contemporary farm complexes. Each farm was centred on a hall, with the date range for its occupation as a farmhouse provided by finds from the associated cluster of sunken featured buildings. Occupation from the fifth into the sixth centuries was centred on halls 1, 2, 3 and 6, while halls 4, 5 and 7 seem to date from the sixth into the seventh centuries. Hall 4 may be the direct successor of Hall 6, Hall 5 of Hall 2 and Hall 7 may be derived from Hall 3, though Hall 1 seems to have no obvious successor among the excavated buildings. By the mid-seventh century, the site was apparently running down, reduced to just two farms based on halls 4 and 7. The problem with this is that it would mean that some halls were occupied for well over 50 years.

If average spans of 30 to 35 years for each generation and building phase are accepted, it may be that a more realistic picture is one of no more than two farm units per generation. In that case, the mid-seventh-century settlement was no smaller than it had been in the fifth and sixth centuries. Estimates of the population in any given generation might range between 20 and 40 individuals, on the basis of up to ten persons per farmhouse. A modern excavation of the nearby contemporary cemetery at West Stow could have provided invaluable information as to its population size. Unfortunately it had already been looted and no proper record kept of the graves from which the surviving objects were removed.

Mucking

Nevertheless the interpretation of West Stow has provided us with a key, which enables us to interpret other settlements on sand or gravel subsoils with large numbers of sunken featured buildings. Mucking (Essex) is one of these, and is an extensive settlement complex occupying a gravel terrace, overlooking the Thames estuary near Tilbury. It was excavated in advance of quarrying in the late 1960s and the early 1970s, and some 210 *Grubenhäuser* and the post-hole plans of about 50 halls were recovered. A full analysis of the different pottery types and other objects, including a coin hoard of the early eighth century, has enabled Helena Hamerow

to demonstrate that particular zones of the settlement were occupied in any given period. These settlement zones represent hamlets, each consisting of individual farm units made up of a hall and a small cluster of associated sunken featured buildings.

An overall date range from within the first half of the fifth century to the early eighth century can be subdivided into a fifth-century phase (A), a fifth- into sixth-century phase (A/B), a sixth- into seventh-century phase (B/C) and a main seventh-century phase (C) ending in the early eighth century. Occupation in period A is restricted to the south-west part of the excavated area directly south of a large cemetery. Phase A/B is located in two separate areas, perhaps two separate hamlets. There is some continuity of occupation into the sixth century within the south-west area of phase A, but also a new zone of settlement directly northeast of the large cemetery. The next phase B/C takes us slightly further north-east again and from the sixth into the seventh century. Finally phase C occupation is more scattered inland to the west, north-west and south-west of the area settled in period B/C.

When looking at the plan of the zones inhabited during successive phases (15), it should not be forgotten that the gentle slope down from the gravel terrace towards the Thames to the east was not excavated at all. It seems reasonable to suggest that the settlement extended down here, particularly in phase A/B with its rather thin and scattered pattern of buildings. These slopes were not about to be destroyed by commercial gravel extraction and their thick soil cover did not reveal any soil-marks or cropmarks to show whether buildings were present there. Consequently there was little to encourage the authorities to fund excavation there.

Returning to the buildings within the excavated zone, there were 67 sunken featured buildings in phase A alone, which equals the total for West Stow. The virtual absence of recorded hall buildings from this area (just two to the north-west) probably reflects practical difficulties in identifying post-holes, which may have only just penetrated into the gravel sub-soil. Also, the excavators were having to work very quickly in advance of large drag-line machines extracting the gravel. Many more halls were identified for the subsequent phases, as the excavation progressed to the north-east

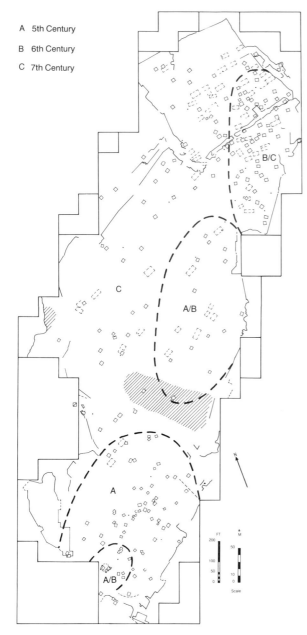

A 5th Century

B 6th Century

C 7th Century

15 *Plan of the Mucking (Essex) cemetery and settlement complex. The settlement has been phased from pottery and other finds in the* Grubenhäuser. *Zone A buildings date to the fifth century, two zones marked A/B from the later fifth into the sixth century, zone B/C from the later sixth into the seventh century and zone C to the seventh and early eighth centuries. These zones imply hamlet-sized settlements based on farm units of a hall and two or more* Grubenhäuser *as at West Stow.*

of area A. Hamerow adopts the West Stow interpretation, seeing each phase as representing a hamlet (or pair of hamlets) lasting around three generations. Each hamlet consisted of several farmsteads, each centred on a hall with an associated cluster of sunken featured buildings, the latter providing the dating evidence. Thus the occupation of phase A/B to the north of the large cemetery had nine halls and 14 sunken featured buildings in a rather dispersed layout, phase B/C had 19 halls and 56 SFBs and the more spread-out phase C produced 21 halls and 56 SFBs.

Full analysis of the two contemporary cemeteries which shared the gravel terrace with these hamlets is not yet complete and only part of Cemetery I amounting to just 50 or so burials was rescued from the quarrying. On the other hand, the large Cemetery II was as thoroughly excavated as possible and produced some 800 burials. On the basis of a conservative estimate of 900 burials over three centuries, with nine generations of 33 years per generation, Hamerow suggests around 100 occupants per generation. She further assumes that there were originally some 65 halls and that each had a 'lifespan' of 40 years, while sunken featured buildings would only last some 20 years. This gives an average of 10 halls and 14 SFBs at any one time, with an average of 10 people occupying each hall. A continual process of settlement shift seems to have been taking place across the site. Replacement timber halls and *Grubenhäuser* were constructed on open farmland by each generation, the old halls being abandoned as soon as the new ones were ready to move into and any reusable timber extracted from them to help construct still more sunken featured buildings. There is also the question of whether this landscape was actually being farmed by Romano-British communities in the later fourth and earlier fifth centuries. The terrace seems to represent an abandoned landscape when the Anglo-Saxons first occupied it, but we do not know what was happening on the slopes down to the river.

Bishopstone

Both Mucking and West Stow begin within the fifth century, while Chalton and Cowdery's Down are centred in the seventh century, with a possible starting point in the later sixth century. So it is not surprising that some people have wondered whether the two Hampshire

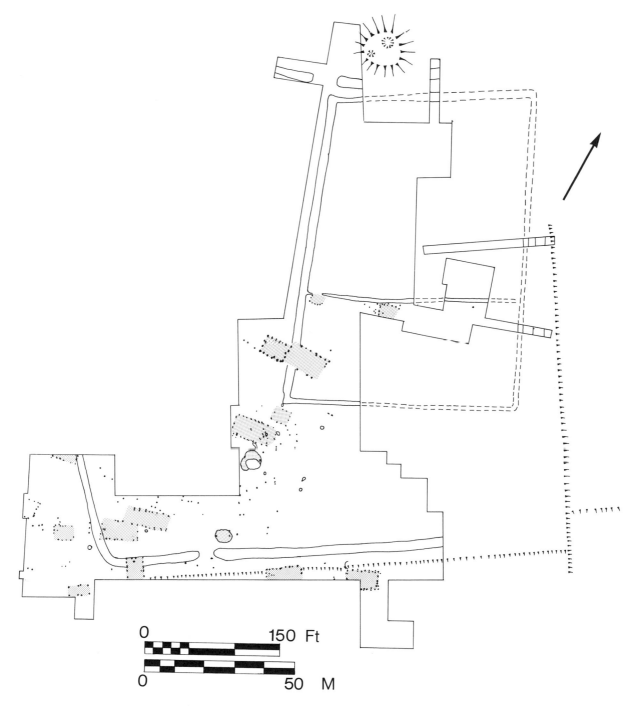

0 150 Ft

0 50 M

downland settlements represent a special type of carefully planned hamlet with fenced farmyards, whose origins are no earlier than the late sixth century. Fortunately the site excavated on Rookery Hill, Bishopstone, in East Sussex reveals that this chalkland settlement

16 *Plan of the central excavated area of the Bishopstone (E. Sussex) settlement with rectangular post-hole buildings, a few short sections of fence enclosures of Chalton type and just two* Grubenhäuser *(out of a total of three). Datable to the fifth and sixth centuries.*

type also occurred in the later fifth century. As at Cowdery's Down, the discovery of this settlement was an unexpected result of a rescue excavation during construction work in 1967-68. It revealed an Anglo-Saxon cemetery of 118 burials datable to the fifth and sixth centuries, which is still not published. This cemetery occupied part of the south-facing slope of a chalk ridge of the South Downs, overlooking the coast between Seaford and the modern Channel ferry port at Newhaven.

A post-hole building appeared in the chalk at one edge of the cemetery and further investigation revealed many more post-holes and pits for sunken featured buildings across the upper slopes of the ridge above the burial ground (**16**). Only three of the 22 buildings excavated were *Grubenhäuser*, but at least two of them contained spindlewhorls associated with cloth production, and the base of the hollow seems to have been the floor. There was just one isolated small trench-based 'hall', which had been destroyed by fire, leaving charcoal traces of horizontal timber beams laid in the trenches as a base for the plank wall framework. The rest of the buildings were rectangular or square post-hole ground-level structures, though one was unusual in having its longer pair of walls slightly bowed out at the centre. This implies that the roof had also been bowed upwards, as it is essential to maintain the same angle for the roof along its entire length, if the rain is to run off effectively.

Sections of fence post-holes were also found, but the plough damage was much greater here than at Chalton, so it proved impossible to reconstruct any of the farm units. Decorated pottery and other finds suggest a date range for the Bishopstone settlement which essentially matches that for its cemetery. The exception is the isolated trench-based hall, which had distinctively different pottery associated with it according to Mark Gardiner, and might represent part of a farm datable to the seventh and eighth centuries. On the other hand, there is nothing to suggest that the settlement in the central excavated area continued into the seventh century. If it had, we would have expected to see a general change from post-hole to trench foundations for the ground-level buildings, as occurred at Chalton and Cowdery's Down. Although part of the settlement was constructed over Roman farm enclosures, the Late Roman farm itself was not

located, so it is not known whether it was still functioning when the Anglo-Saxon settlement was founded. Its excavator has estimated that there may have been a total of around 60 buildings occupied over a period of between 100 and 150 years. So over four or even five generations this would represent a settlement of comparable size to Chalton, with three or four farm units.

Settlements in the Anglo-Saxon homelands

It is time to turn to the settlements of the continental homelands of the Anglo-Saxons in the Netherlands, north Germany and Denmark, looking at the rich archaeological evidence from large-scale excavations there. These leave no doubt that the concept of an organized fenced farmyard as the basic unit of settlement was well established long before the migrations to Britain. For example, the Dutch inland site at Wijster, the German site of Flögeln-Eekhöltjen (**17**) and the Danish site at Vorbasse (Jutland) were all settlements organized in rectangular or square fenced plots. All three were abandoned in the first half or around the middle of the fifth century. In the case of Vorbasse, we know of a sixth-century successor settlement nearby, which suggests that at least a part of its population did not leave. No such immediate successors are known for Wijster or Flögeln, however, and it may well be that overpopulation, combined with soil exhaustion of their fields, prompted their abandonment and the search for new land elsewhere.

The *Grubenhaus* is the one building type which is exactly the same whether excavated in a continental or an English Anglo-Saxon settlement. Loomweights, spindlewhorls and other debris associated with craftwork imply that manufacturing was one of the main activities for which they were used. Animals could also be tethered inside them and there is evidence for this both at Flögeln and West Stow. Continental archaeologists view them as workshops and general ancillary buildings, but certainly not as human dwellings. At the same

17 *Plan of the Flögeln-Eekhöltjen (Germany) settlement in the second and third centuries* AD *organized into large rectangular fenced farmyards containing long hall-houses with cattle stalls, granaries based on post-holes,* Grubenhäuser *and wells.*

Flögeln−Eekhöltjen 1971−1975

time, the continental equivalent to English halls are massive byre-houses. In these at least half of the building was subdivided into stalls, designed to keep cattle and other livestock in good condition through the relatively severe winters of these regions.

Cattle stalling seems to have been unnecessary in England with its mild, wet climate. The nearest thing to cattle stalls yet seen in an excavated Early Anglo-Saxon settlement is the set of four or more small buildings with a row of central posts at Chalton. But these were nothing like as impressive as the double lines of internal posts which carried the roof of a continental byre-house with its wickerwork stall divisions and wooden drains placed either side of a central walkway down the length of the byre.

Well-preserved buildings of this type have been excavated at Feddersen Wierde near Bremerhaven (Germany) (18) and many other settlements on the coastal margins of northwest Germany and the Netherlands. Damp soil conditions there preserved the timber walls, roof supports and floors of these three-aisled-hall-houses (*Dreischiffigeshallenhäuser*) as the Germans call them. A typical width was 6m (20ft), but they vary in length according to how many stalls they contained. For example, one hall-house in Feddersen Wierde with ten pairs of stalls was 25m (82ft) long. In the inland sites such as Flögeln these survive as no more than stains in the sand or gravel, indicating where timber posts and planks had rotted in the ground. So the timber and wattlework of the coastal settlements allow us to reconstruct the inland buildings with great accuracy. The living area for the humans was at the opposite end to the byre and separated from it by a partitioned corridor. This ran across the width of the building with the main doors at either side, while there was usually a separate doorway at the far end of the byre for the animals.

The founders of the coastal settlements had taken advantage of a temporary lowering of the sea level between the period around the birth of Christ and their enforced abandonment of these marginal areas in the fifth century at the time of the Anglo-Saxon migration. Temporary seasonal camps for cattle herdsmen were replaced by small settlements consisting of hall-houses, each accompanied by a small grain store raised clear of the ground on four or more posts to keep its contents dry. These

were built directly on the dry land surface and at Feddersen Wierde each hall-house was aligned east-west on a natural low sandy island behind the shelter of a barrier beach. Later in the first century, a rise in sea levels brought floods and after this the settlement had to be raised artificially out of flood range.

Earlier buildings were buried under mounds of clay and animal dung, so that each new hall-house and granary stood on a platform which entombed the low walls and floor of its predecessor. These individual mounds coalesced over time into one large artificial island mound, which the Dutch call a *Terp* and the Germans a *Wurt* or *Wierde*. In order to maximize the number of buildings on the mound, the hall-houses were positioned as close as possible to their neighbours, radiating outwards like the spokes of a wheel. Each byre-house and its accompanying buildings were enclosed by a ditch or a fence, clearly demarcating its property from that of its neighbours (19). Of course, the sea eventually won the battle, making agriculture impossible, but it was not until the mid-fifth century or a little later that Feddersen Wierde was deserted. So deeply buried were some of its buildings under mound platforms that the only element not preserved is the roof.

Due allowance must be made for the poor quality of the timber used at Feddersen Wierde and the probability that the inland settlements had better access to woodland and may have been built with more timber and less wattling than the coastal settlements. Nevertheless we can use the well-preserved evidence from Feddersen Wierde to reconstruct the buildings of inland settlements such as Flögeln or Wijster. The fenced enclosures of the inland sites were of course much larger, for there was no special reason to restrict their size, as there was on coastal mounds. Even the living areas of the continental byre-houses were considerably larger than the biggest halls at Chalton, but then they were also at least 1m (3¼ft) wider.

Feddersen Wierde and other sites did contain some smaller rectangular buildings without byres, measuring 7m (23ft) by 5m (16ft), which are interpreted as belonging to craftsmen. But these still used internal aisle posts to support the roof timbers, whereas the Cowdery's Down halls took the weight of the roof through their crucks, door frames and the low-set plank walls. The living-areas of some Wijster byre-houses seem to be moving towards the English form of

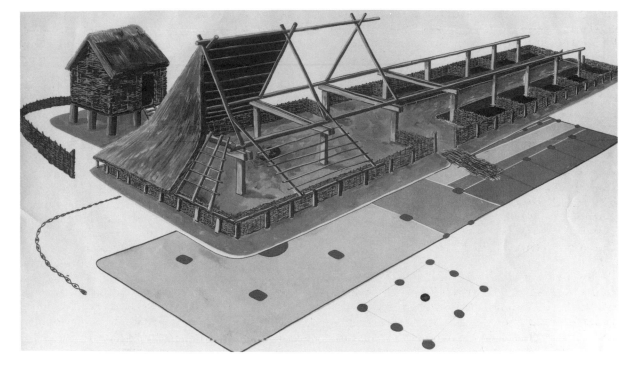

18 *Reconstruction of a three-aisled-hall-house at Feddersen Wierde (Germany). The timbers and wattling of the walls and partitions were preserved in the damp soil conditions with the weight of the roof supported by two rows of internal wooden posts forming a nave and two aisles. A living area around a hearth is in the foreground and there are cattle stalls beyond. Hay and other winter fodder may have been stored in the roof above the stalls. Next door is a small building on wooden stilts to store dry grain.*

construction. The inner roof posts have been moved out to the wall line and presumably are replaced by timbers curved inwards, either as true cruck frames or as supports for a cross-beam called a base-cruck. This had the advantage of allowing more space around the central hearth, so that people could avoid bumping into roof-support aisle posts.

If Anglo-Saxon halls can be seen as the English equivalents of continental hall-houses, without the byres which were simply not necessary, why have archaeologists over here regarded *Grubenhäuser* as dwellings? Why was the excavator of West Stow determined to reconstruct sunken featured buildings as elaborate buildings almost as large as the halls?

Sutton Courtenay

The answer can be traced back to the pioneering excavations of E.T. Leeds at Sutton Courtenay (now in Oxfordshire) in the 1920s and 1930s (**20**). When Leeds visited the gravel quarries there, he recognized and dug out the darker soil, pottery and other objects which filled the hollows of former *Grubenhäuser*. But he had to fit this work between his duties at the Ashmolean Museum in Oxford, so he was reliant on the quarrymen who extracted gravel by hand with pick and shovel. He asked them to reserve areas which produced the tell-tale dark soil stains hidden under the topsoil cover until he was next able to visit. Presumably he will have seen only relatively small areas of the gravel surface fully exposed from its cover of ploughsoil at any one visit. It is not surprising then that he failed to interpret the two patterns of post-holes he recorded and planned as parts of two halls; instead he regarded them as small and unimportant sheds.

The fills of the *Grubenhäuser*, with their domestic debris of pottery, loomweights, textile production implements and even a fine, though damaged fifth-century silver-gilt equal-arm brooch, convinced Leeds that they were used as dwellings and not simply workshops. He contrasted the relative sophistication and

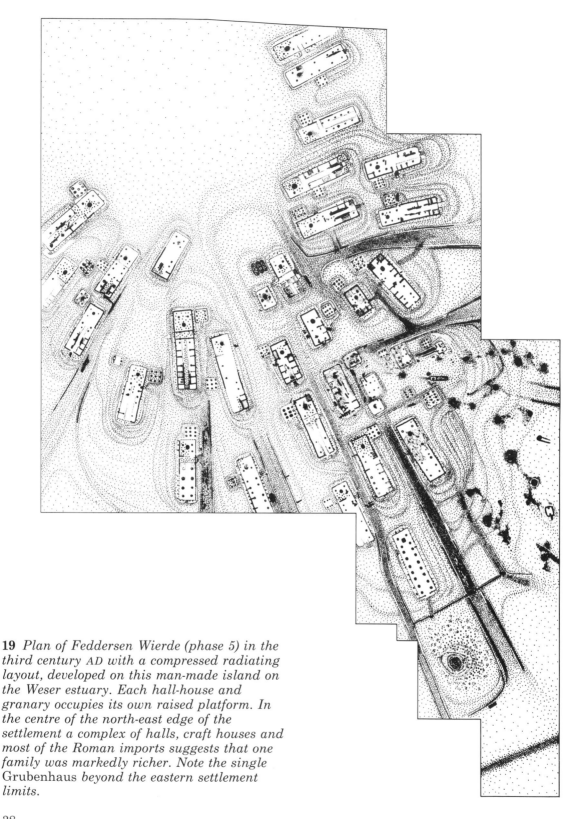

19 *Plan of Feddersen Wierde (phase 5) in the third century* AD *with a compressed radiating layout, developed on this man-made island on the Weser estuary. Each hall-house and granary occupies its own raised platform. In the centre of the north-east edge of the settlement a complex of halls, craft houses and most of the Roman imports suggests that one family was markedly richer. Note the single* Grubenhaus *beyond the eastern settlement limits.*

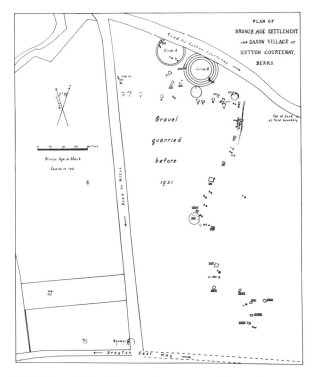

PLAN OF
BRONZE AGE SETTLEMENT
AND SAXON VILLAGE AT
SUTTON COURTENAY,
BERKS.

20 *Plan of the Sutton Courtenay (Oxon.)
settlement as excavated and recorded by E. T.
Leeds. The area in the centre marked
destroyed was removed by gravel digging. Dots
representing post-holes forming a rectangle
immediately S of Circle B and a similar right-
angle of dots (Building XXII) halfway down
the east side of the site were probably two halls
of Chalton or West Stow post-hole type. Each
hall seems to have a cluster of* Grubenhäuser
nearby as at Mucking and West Stow.

wealth of the objects accompanying the burials
in contemporary Anglo-Saxon cemeteries, with
what he took to be the squalor of the people's
living conditions. His interpretation dominated
the ideas of most English field archaeologists
up until the 1970s, when the role of the hall as
the principal farmhouse became obvious. We
can now see that the Sutton Courtenay settlement fits the West Stow and Mucking model
with an apparent cluster of sunken featured
buildings associated with each of the two halls.

Catholme
Not all settlements on gravel and sand terraces
and ridges conform to this pattern, though
the majority do so. An exception occurs at

Catholme (Staffordshire) in the Trent valley.
Some sunken featured buildings were excavated here, but they form a minority in a hamlet
divided into farmyard enclosures by hedges and
ditches (**21**). A wide range of building types was
found, including both post-hole and trench-
based ground-level rectangular structures. One
of the most interesting aspects is a marked
similarity between these and some timber buildings excavated on a third-century Romano-
British enclosed farmstead at Dunston's Clump
(in Nottinghamshire) (**22**). Unfortunately the
Catholme settlement produced virtually no
artefacts and has been dated from radiocarbon
samples. These seem to imply a date range
between the fifth and ninth centuries, perhaps
centred on the seventh to eighth centuries.

Assuming that the Dunston's Clump site has
been correctly dated to the Roman period, we
may be observing the contribution of a Romano-
British peasant building tradition to the repertoire of buildings found in Anglo-Saxon settlements (**23**). Indeed the occupants of Catholme
may have been native British farmers who had
adopted some aspects of Anglo-Saxon material
culture from their new neighbours. Our problem is that we still know remarkably little from
excavation about the ordinary rural settlements of Roman Britain below the rank of
villas. This makes it very difficult to assess
what sort of contribution the British may have
made to the development of the hall buildings
found in Early Anglo-Saxon settlements.

Livestock
We must now turn briefly to examine the
archaeological evidence for farming in both
continental and English settlements. Animal
bone was very well preserved at Feddersen
Wierde and it would seem that cattle ownership
was particularly significant. Quantity seems to
have been more important than the quality of
the small animals and there is no sign of
selective breeding to improve the stock. Cattle
formed 48.3 per cent of domestic animals, followed by 23.7 per cent sheep (or goat), 12.7 per
cent horses, 11.1 per cent pigs and 4.2 per cent
dogs. This can be compared to figures for the
West Stow animal bones of between 34.3 per
cent and 36.3 per cent for cattle, 44.4 per cent
and 50 per cent for sheep (or goat), 13.7 per
cent and 19.7 per cent pigs. These imply that
while sheep were more numerous, cattle were
the prime source of meat at West Stow.

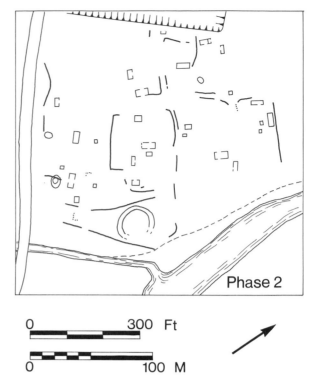

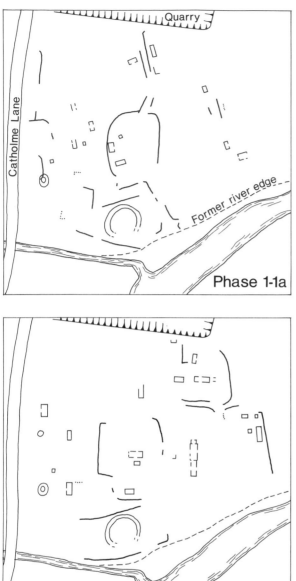

21 *Plans of the first three phases of the Catholme (Staffs.) settlement. Ditched, hedged and fenced enclosures divided it into farm units of rectangular timber buildings and a few* Grubenhäuser. *Dating is dependent on radiocarbon dates, which suggest the seventh and eighth centuries.*

deer bones. The milder climate and the existing balance between sheep flocks and cattle herds in the Late Roman landscape of lowland Britain must be presumed to underlie this apparent diminution of the importance of cattle in Anglo-Saxon animal husbandry after the migrations. Nevertheless it was a cow that was deliberately sacrificed and deposited in a pit close to one of the largest halls at Cowdery's Down.

Agriculture

Crops grown at Feddersen Wierde were dominated by barley and oats, which made up 40 per cent, while beans and flax each formed 25 per cent of the total. Barley was important for the making of ale and recurs as a significant crop on English settlements at Bishopstone, Chalton,

The West Stow figures are supported by other sites such as Bishopstone with cattle at 25 per cent, sheep at 39 per cent, pig 17 per cent and horse 2 per cent. Unfortunately no published analysis of the animal bone from Chalton has yet appeared. Sheep, cattle and pig were all present, probably in similar proportions to those at West Stow and Bishopstone. Oysters were gathered from the coast near Chalton, but the evidence for hunting at this or any other site is very limited, though there were some

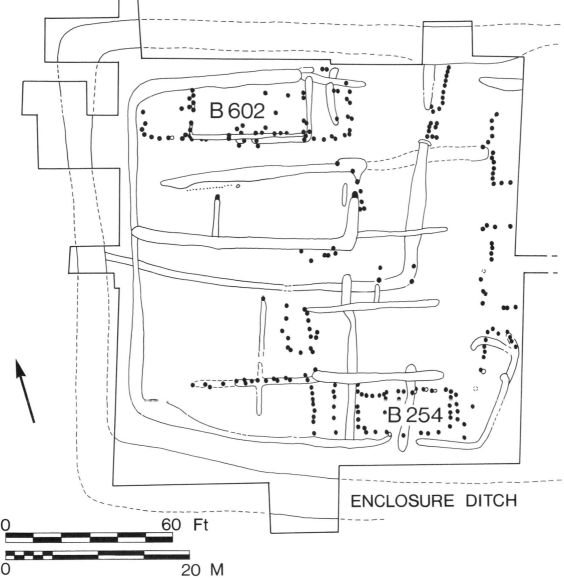

22 *Plan of a Romano-British farmstead within a ditched enclosure at Dunston's Clump (Notts.).*

Cowdery's Down and West Stow. On the other hand, spelt wheat and rye seem to be more important at West Stow and oats were also present there. Rye is a particularly hardy cereal which thrives in relatively poor soil conditions and was also a significant crop in the late phases of the Flögeln settlement. Most of Feddersen Wierde's crops were probably planted on the adjacent barrier beach, but ploughmarks have also been traced on the settlement mound, made by a true plough with a mould board needed for turning heavy clay soil.

On the lighter soils of the sandy inland regions of the continental homelands a more primitive type of plough called an ard was used. Two of these wooden implements were

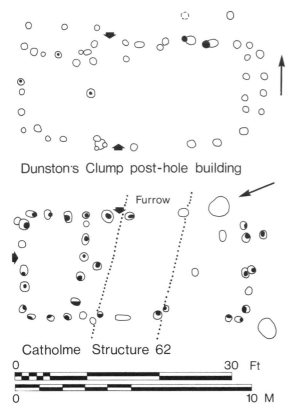

Dunston's Clump post-hole building

Catholme Structure 62

23 *Comparative plans of Catholme Building 62 and Dunston's Clump B254 suggest that a British timber building tradition may have contributed to the Early Anglo-Saxon hall, or could the Catholme settlement represent a largely British community?*

recovered intact from the Flögeln site, as were the small rectangular fields they had been used to plough. One of the graves in an isolated cluster at Sutton Hoo (Suffolk) appears to have contained a wooden ard and a ploughman placed as if running with it. This type of implement cuts a simple shallow furrow, so it was normal to plough once in one direction and then replough at right angles across the first set of furrows. Hence the ideal field shape was a square or rectangle. Such fields also existed in prehistoric and Roman Britain and the Chalton settlement was built over such a field system. They are commonly called 'Celtic fields', an unfortunate term as their origins lie in the Late Neolithic and Early Bronze Age; here they will be referred to as co-axial fields.

So the farming technology of the Anglo-Saxons on the Continent was very similar to that of the Romano-British farmers. The new-comers seem to have taken over existing field systems, while a milder climate and a landscape perhaps better suited to sheep rearing may have seen sheep replace cattle as the most numerous animal kept on Anglo-Saxon farms. Nevertheless cattle remained an important resource for Anglo-Saxon communities providing milk and meat, as well as hides and horns. As there was no need to keep livestock indoors throughout the English winter, their halls seem rather modest in scale after their continental equivalents. Still, the living space in the larger halls of Chalton or West Stow was substantial when compared to modern house living rooms.

4

Estate centres

All the sites discussed so far were excavated on either sand and gravels or chalkland. Sand and gravel provide the best air photography evidence for settlements, and archaeologists are now reasonably confident of their ability to recognize the dark blobs of *Grubenhäuser* on them. Hall-type buildings can occasionally be seen from the air (see **26-29**), but do not often show up clearly. This leaves a wide range of other soil types and extensive areas of England which have yet to produce evidence for an Early Anglo-Saxon settlement.

Soil accumulation in the base of valleys can bury sites under many metres of soil. Settlements here will only be detected by chance and the three *Grubenhäuser* found near Botolphs parish church in West Sussex were the unexpected result of an excavation there. Other downland valley sites have yet to be located in Sussex, as have the settlements of the coastal plain brickearths there. The distribution of contemporary Anglo-Saxon cemeteries provides some guide as to where we might expect to find associated settlements. On the other hand, the cemeteries themselves were often found by chance and are not an ideal indicator.

It would seem that Anglo-Saxon farmers normally lived in small hamlets consisting of no more than a few individual farmsteads. They may also have lived in isolated farms, which probably looked much like the individual farm units of these hamlets. Certainly there is no evidence as yet for larger settlements which could be described as villages. So where did their rulers, who appear in the written record from the seventh century as kings and princes, have their residences and how did these differ from the hamlets of Chalton and West Stow?

Yeavering

Heroic poetry such as *Beowulf* portrays these rulers enjoying the company of their warriors and feasting with them in great halls. The identification of a site containing large rectangular buildings at Yeavering in Northumberland and its subsequent excavation in the 1950s and early 1960s provided us with our first view of these great halls. There is every reason to believe that this settlement is the same one briefly described by Bede as the former royal *villa* called *ad Gefrin*.

The context of this reference was a visit made to the villa by Edwin, king of the Northumbrians, shortly after his formal conversion to Catholic Christianity in the late 620s. He was accompanied by his queen, a Kentish princess who was already a Christian when she married him. A missionary bishop called Paulinus had travelled north with her from Kent and played a leading role in persuading Edwin and his advisers to accept the faith. The royal visit to *ad Gefrin* lasted 36 days and apparently throughout it Paulinus was fully occupied in catechizing the local population and baptizing them in the river Glen nearby.

Of course Bede was writing about 100 years after this visit, but his record of events in the seventh century, especially those in his own kingdom of Northumbria, is generally regarded as reasonably accurate. In this particular passage, he goes on to comment that in the time of subsequent kings, the villa of *ad Gefrin* was abandoned and another built at *Maelmin*. The similarity of Bede's name of *ad Gefrin* to the modern place-name of Yeavering and the proximity of the excavated settlement on a prominent hillock immediately above the river Glen leaves little room for doubt that Edwin's villa stood here. Air photography has also located the probable site of its successor of *Maelmin* at Milfield.

Long delays in the publication of the full report of the Yeavering excavations, written

24 *Phase plans of Yeavering (Northumberland).* Top left: *centred on Hall A2 probably built for Æthelfrith (592–616) next to the cattle enclosure (Phase IIIA/B);* Top right: *centred on Hall A4 probably built for Edwin (616–32) with a wooden grandstand (Phase IIIC);* Bottom left: *centred on Hall A3a probably built for Oswald (633–41) with a possible church (Hall B) constructed after the demolition of the cattle enclosure and grandstand (Phase IV);* Bottom right: *centred on Hall A3b probably built for Oswiu (641–70) (Phase V).*

by Brian Hope-Taylor in the early 1960s, but not appearing until 1977, meant that many aspects of it were already out of date. Nevertheless it marked an important watershed in the development of British archaeological technique. The principles of area excavation and the careful identification and dissection of overlying timber buildings were successfully applied here.

Areas A and B were the key elements for the interpretation of the site. A sequence of hall buildings was constructed in Area A, beginning with modest post-hole and later trench-built halls (A5-8) of the same size as those at Chalton, West Stow and Mucking (**24**). Subsequently a massive hall (A2) was built here, succeeded on an adjacent site by another still larger (A4). Hall A4 was paired with a smaller hall (A1a), but then a major fire destroyed both halls and damaged or burnt down other buildings

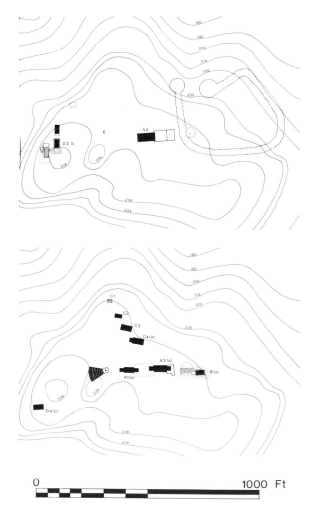

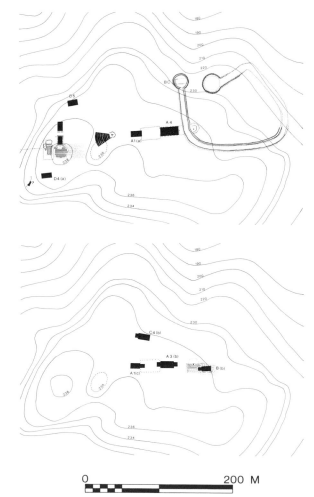

across the settlement.

This was not the end of the sequence for another large hall was built in place of A4 (A3a), again paired with a smaller hall (A1b). When these in turn were destroyed by fire, they were rebuilt once again (A3b and A1c). At some later stage, probably within a generation, the settlement at Yeavering seems to have been abandoned and interestingly one of the great halls revealed by air photography at Milfield has a similar layout to Yeavering's Hall A3.

Area B lies immediately to the east of Area A and includes part of a great timber-walled enclosure, interpreted as a cattle corral. This Great Enclosure has been described in the past as a fort, but the absence of an external ditch enclosing the palisades mean that it would be vulnerable to attack by a well-organized warband. It does seem more likely to be a place to protect livestock from wild animals and rustlers. This enclosure was deliberately demolished after the first fire which destroyed halls A4 and A1a.

Other complexes of buildings were located and excavated, notably in areas C, D and E, but none of these represent such a long sequence of occupation as areas A and B combined. Their buildings have been related to those of the Area A sequence in terms of whether they were affected by one or other of two fires, which respectively destroyed halls A4 and A3a. As the wind was blowing in completely opposite directions when each of these fires occurred, it was possible to differentiate between them. The excavator also related these sequences to changing construction methods in building the timber halls within Area A. The results seem to imply a fairly ordinary rural settlement initially, whose buildings were first constructed in post-holes and then adopted a plank-in-trench construction. The whole character of the settlement then changed dramatically with the construction of the first of the great halls (A2) with a length of nearly 25m (82ft) and a width of 11m (36ft).

This seems to mark the point in time when a royal villa was established here (**colour plate 1**). Its function was to provide suitable short-term accommodation for the king and his household. There, perhaps once, or at most twice a year they would briefly reside and doubtless engage in such aristocratic pursuits as hunting during the day. They would feast each evening on the food-rents owed to the king by the farmers of the surrounding region. This primitive form of taxation was essential in an economy which lacked coinage and the ability readily to turn food products into coin or bullion as in a market economy.

Livestock brought in on the hoof could be kept safe until needed for consumption within the Great Enclosure. Barrels and sacks of food and drink could be stored temporarily in barns which might prove difficult for the archaeologist to distinguish from halls. There would not necessarily be sufficient space in the halls to house the entire royal retinue and we should imagine some of them occupying tents in the open spaces between the complexes of timber buildings.

The king would have as many such centres as he had major estates and he and his household would constantly travel from one royal estate to the next. His visit to any individual villa would therefore be periodic, once or twice a year at most, and if the king or his queen did not happen to visit a villa in any particular year, we might suppose that the inhabitants of the associated region could keep the livestock and the produce they owed for that year. By such means the pretence could be maintained that these renders were hospitality willingly offered by the king's men, rather than tribute owed by dependent subjects or a defeated enemy. At the same time as providing for the feeding of the king and his household, these estate centres performed other valuable social functions. Above all they provided a means of access for the people to their king, enabling him to sit in judgement and settle disputes.

Other types of royal centre

The account given in the *Life of St Wilfrid* of another Northumbrian king called Ecgfrith proceeding around his kingdom with much pomp and feasting rather later in the seventh century makes it clear that villas of the Yeavering and Milfield type represent the most commonplace and least important royal centres. At the top of the hierarchy were the sites described in Latin both as *civitas* and *urbs* such as Bamburgh, a coastal strongpoint fortified by the British and subsequently acquired by a Northumbrian king called Ida around the middle of the sixth century. Further south in England former Roman walled towns such as York and Canterbury, many of which had enjoyed the status of *civitates*, with a role as regional centres under the Roman administration, functioned as important royal centres in the seventh and later centuries. As yet no archaeological remains have been located in any of these places which could be regarded as parts of a royal palace complex, perhaps because in many cases their remains may well have been destroyed by the expansion of later cathedral church buildings.

An Anglo-Saxon *civitas* was a particularly important type of *urbs*, but next down the scale came an *urbs* which was not a *civitas*, such as Dunbar. These 'cities' or 'citadels' may also have contained royal buildings visited more often or for longer periods during the year by the king and his household than was the case with the rural villas. A royal official at Dunbar, described as a *praefectus*, resided there to look after the king's interests in that region during the rest of the year. Royal agents of less exalted rank would also be needed at the royal villas to open, clean and if necessary repair the timber halls in preparation for a royal visit and ensure that the food renders were gathered by the required time.

A special structure which for the present is unique to Yeavering was excavated in Area E of the site. It appears to be a curved wooden grandstand, enlarged once by the addition of further tiers at the back, which doubled its seating capacity. The nearest comparable structures are the stone theatres of the Roman world and it would seem to represent a small segment of such a theatre constructed entirely in wood. As this grandstand was slightly damaged, but not destroyed, by the first fire, its construction may well date to the same period as the building of Hall A4 and certainly it is unlikely to have been built any earlier than the first of the great halls (A2).

The dating of Yeavering

So what are the dates of these great halls and the grandstand and to whose reigns should they be assigned? Very few objects were recovered from the settlement and of those only two were datable items of metalwork. One was an iron buckle loop inlaid with silver wire recovered from one of the dumps of debris associated with the demolition of the Great Enclosure in Area B. This demolition followed the damage caused by the first of the two major fires. The buckle may well have been lost or thrown away in the period of occupation which preceded this fire,

that is in phase IIIc centred on halls A4, A1a and the grandstand.

Interestingly this buckle had been imported across the English Channel. Similar buckles were buried in graves dating between c.570-80 and c.630-40 in the Frankish world (present-day northern France, Belgium and western Germany). The excavator suggested that the first fire occurred as part of a devastation of Northumbria in 632-3 by Edwin's enemies. This was recorded by Bede, though he did not specifically mention *ad Gefrin* in this context. Edwin's opponents were a Christian Welsh prince and the pagan Anglo-Saxon ruler of the north Midlands kingdom called Mercia. Once they had killed Edwin in battle, they were free to ravage Northumbria. As a Frankish buckle of the type found at Yeavering might have been brought north by a man serving in the household of Edwin's Kentish bride in the 620s, the excavator might be correct about the date of the fire, though it is not possible to be certain.

The other datable object is a Frankish coin, a gilt copper alloy fake copying a gold coin issued by a moneyer at Huy, in present-day Belgium. When and where this forgery was made is not known, but the coins it copied were issued in the 630s or 640s. The fake had been lost in Hall A3b during the final phase of occupation at Yeavering and after the second fire. The excavator again suggested an historical context for that fire: the series of punitive attacks mounted on Northumbria between c.651 and 655 by the same Mercian king who twenty years earlier had killed Edwin in battle. It is quite possible that a copy of a coin minted in the 630s to 640s might have been lost in the late 650s or the 660s, but that is as far as we can go in our interpretation.

The dating of fire destructions by reference to campaigns described in general terms by Bede, who never mentions Yeavering by name in connection with these events, is clearly a risky business. After all, fires can be the result of accidents, or might be used deliberately but peacefully as a means of demolishing redundant timber buildings. Still, the two datable objects do suggest that Hope-Taylor's historical estimates may be not too far from reality.

So it would seem likely that halls A4 and A1a, together with the grandstand may well belong to Edwin's reign. If that is the case, then Hall A2 may have been built for the king overthrown by Edwin on his return from exile in East Anglia, a man called Æthelfrith. The grandstand might have been built originally for Æthelfrith, if we see it as a place where royal decisions were announced. On the other hand, its construction fits rather better the needs of Bishop Paulinus as a place where he could preach through an interpreter to the local pagan population, before leading these individuals down to the river for a rather chilly baptism. Paulinus was a member of Augustine's mission from Rome to England and he could even have suggested the idea of constructing a grandstand for this very purpose. Edwin may have sent orders that it be built in advance of the arrival of his royal party and the additions to it could have been tacked on at the back during the royal stay, when the original stand proved to be too small.

Certainly Hope-Taylor's attempts to make the construction of structure E even earlier than the phase including Hall A2 seem difficult to substantiate. After all, earthfast planking is unlikely to last much longer than 50 years, yet those who set fire to it in 632-3 apparently failed to achieve more than superficial damage to it. If we could locate and excavate a royal *vicus* mentioned by Bede at Catterick in Yorkshire, we might well find another wooden grandstand there. Apparently Paulinus visited Catterick with Edwin and baptized the local population in the Swale, presumably not too far from the river cataracts which gave Catterick its Latin name (*Cataractonium*). This would help to confirm the hypothesis that grandstand E at Yeavering was indeed constructed for Paulinus. For the moment it must remain a unique and interesting timber structure.

If Hall A2 belonged to Æthelfrith and A1a, A4 and E to Edwin, then A1b and A3a should have been used by Æthelfrith's heirs, the brothers Oswald and Oswin, who seized control after a period of anarchy following Edwin's death. Presumably it was Oswy who had halls A1c and A3b built after the second fire. The A3 halls were constructed in a markedly different manner from their predecessors A4 and A2. None of them have the two rows of internal posts to support crossbeams below the roof as in A2 and A4. Their timber walls are made from thinner planking set into trenches, whereas the A2 and A4 walls have spaced timbers suggesting a construction method like that found in Cowdery's Down C9 (see **5**). The A3 halls also

have annexes at one or both ends, which are narrower than the width of the main hall, whereas the A2 and A4 halls have internal partitioned areas at either end which are the same width as the hall.

The excavator used these differences to help him assign some of the smaller halls outside Area A to a particular phase of occupation. Thus the series of four buildings, which includes a *Grubenhaus* with timber lining in Area C, was assigned to the period of the two A3 halls because of their thinner plank walls and the presence of narrower annexes attached to some of them. A great hall with annexes of this type also shows up clearly as a cropmark on air photographs of the so-far unexcavated successor settlement of Milfield.

Cowdery's Down and other estate centres
The comparison with Cowdery's Down, both in terms of building technique and also in terms of the large halls, especially C12, which would only just have fitted inside Yeavering A4, raises the question of the status of other sites with such buildings. Are they all royal centres or should we look for other alternative explanations? The only sites located by archaeologists which are also reasonably well documented as being royal villas in the seventh to eighth centuries occur at Yeavering and Milfield. Yet the list of settlements which have produced great halls on the Yeavering scale is steadily growing.

Air photographs have revealed a complex of buildings including halls with annexes at Sprouston in the Tweed valley not far from Yeavering (**25**); two halls at Atcham in Shropshire, one of which had annexes (**26**); other halls at Hatton Rock near Stratford-on-Avon (**27**); Long Itchington near Warwick; Cowage Farm, Foxley near Malmesbury in Wiltshire; and Drayton (**28**) and Long Wittenham (**29**) in the Thames valley near Oxford. Small-scale excavations have tested the dating of the sites at Hatton Rock and Cowage Farm, while more complete excavations were carried out by Brian Hope-Taylor on Doon Hill near Dunbar (**30**), by John Williams at Northampton (**31**) and of course at Cowdery's Down. The latest discovery is being excavated at Yarnton just north of Oxford. Of all these sites only that at Long Itchington might have a royal connection, being mentioned as a royal estate in a document dated to the tenth century.

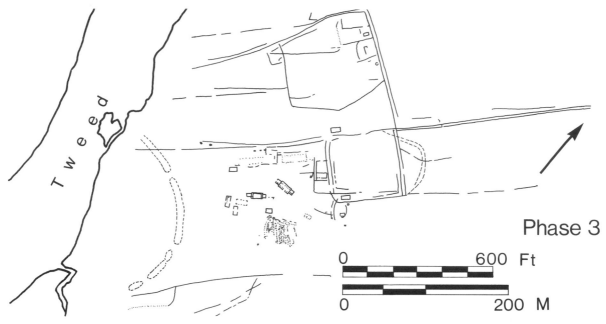

Phase 3

0   600 Ft

0   200 M

25 *Plan of the Sprouston settlement identified from air photos beside the river Tweed. There are two large rectangular halls with narrow square annexes at each end, which resemble the great halls of Yeavering phases IV-V and suggest a date in the seventh or eighth century. A small cemetery immediately to the east may be associated.*

26 *Air photo of two great halls with narrow annexes at Atcham (Shropshire), comparable to those at Yeavering and Sprouston. (Cambridge University Collection: copyright reserved.)*

27 *Air photo of a group of large rectangular halls and a possible church (bottom left corner) at Hatton Rock (Warwicks.). The Anglo-Saxon attribution has been confirmed by pottery and other finds recovered from pipe trenches dug across the site. (Cambridge University Collection: copyright reserved.)*

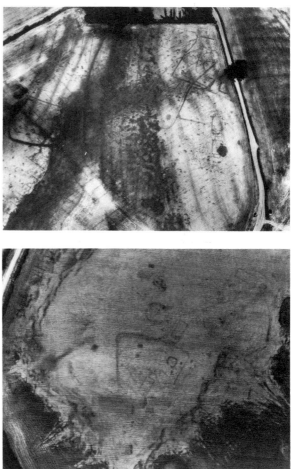

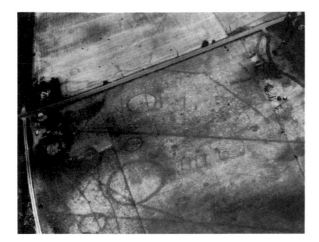

28 *Air photo of a group of great rectangular halls at Drayton (Oxon.), not far from the Sutton Courtenay settlement. The largest hall partially cuts across the prehistoric ring ditch close to the road near the middle of the picture. Like most of halls it is set E-W, but two buildings are aligned N-S. (Cambridge University Collection: copyright reserved.)*

29 *Air photo of a group of three large halls, one of which appears to have bowed-out walls located close to the Early Anglo-Saxon cemetery at Long Wittenham (Oxon.). (Cambridge University Collection: copyright reserved.)*

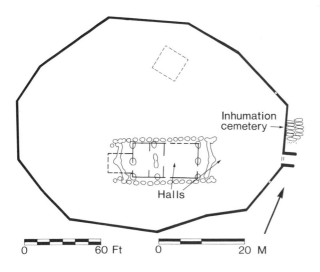

30 *Plan of two successive great halls set within a polygonal fenced enclosure on top of Doon Hill, near Dunbar. The second version has a narrow annexe at one end resembling those on halls of Yeavering phases IV-V. There is a small associated burial ground to the east.*

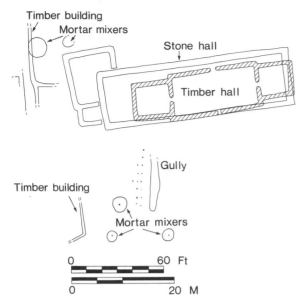

31 *Plan showing a great timber hall with narrow annexes replaced by a still larger stone hall immediately east of St Peter's Church in Northampton. The timber hall can be compared to the Yeavering halls of phases IV and V and its stone successor to royal halls built in France and Germany for Charlemagne and his successors in the eighth and ninth centuries.*

Only a single hall with an annexe was excavated at Doon Hill, but this was apparently the direct successor of an earlier hall which the excavator suggests had been built by the former British owner. When the Northumbrian Angles took over this region, one of them had a hall built in the same manner as those found in the last two phases at Yeavering. At Northampton careful excavation has revealed a large timber hall with an annexe at either end. This was succeeded by a stone-built hall as part of a larger complex of stone buildings, extending under the present church of St Peter located immediately to the west. Radiocarbon dates give a date of AD 840 ± 60 for the demolition of the timber hall and the construction of the stone successor. This is interpreted as meaning perhaps a mid-eighth-century date for the building of the timber hall and an early ninth-century date for the one in stone.

It is certainly tempting to interpret the North-ampton stone hall as part of a monastery or minster church complex based on the predecessor of the present church. If that is the case, was the timber hall the residence of the abbot and the place where he entertained important visitors and delivered justice to those who worked his estates? Certainly this seems to be as satisfactory an explanation as to see it as a royal hall, for which king is supposed to have ever resided here? Northampton is not known from any document as a royal centre at this time and honoured royal visitors could equally well be East Anglian or else Mercian kings from the Trent Valley.

Then what is to be made of the complex of large timber halls built to the west of two small farmyards in phase 4C at Cowdery's Down (**4** and **32**) and then destroyed by fire? Should we attribute these halls to a West Saxon king or sub-king on the basis of the radiocarbon and thermoluminescence dates? If so, should we also try to find a suitable battle or power struggle to explain its violent destruction in the principal record of the deeds of its kings, the *Anglo-Saxon Chronicle*? Perhaps instead we should remember that the primary function of the royal villas was as estate centres. All land belonged ultimately to the king and rents in the form of food or services were owed in return for the right to farm it. In return the king protected his kingdom from its enemies and interceded with the gods of the pagan world for its well-being.

One way a king could reward the warriors who served him, apart from giving them gold and other treasure, or weapons, armour and horses, was to grant them land. This enabled them to marry, settle and raise a family, which would provide the loyal warriors of the future. Parts of the royal estate could be granted over strictly limited periods for this purpose. Grants of one, sometimes two or three, lifetimes were mentioned when such grants come to be recorded in writing. At the end of that period, the estate returned to the king, perhaps to be regranted, but not necessarily so. The warrior receiving such a grant acquired not so much the land itself, which continued to be farmed by others as before, but rather the food-rents and services owed to the king. He would need a hall in which to feast when he came to visit his estate between attending the king on royal business. His wife and children might well reside there in his absence.

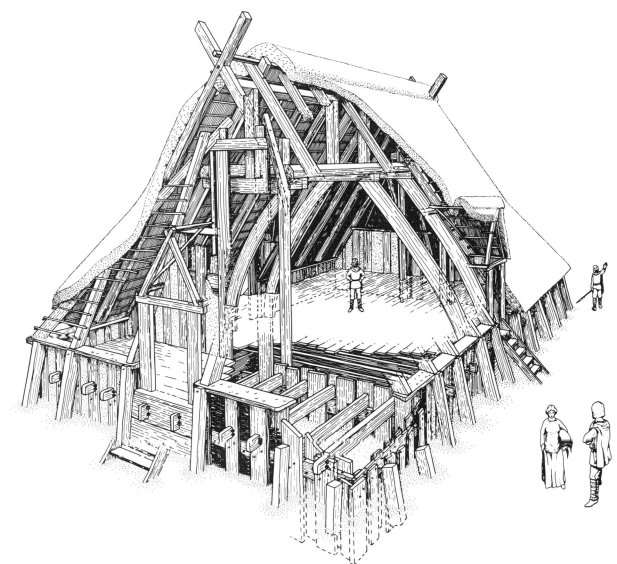

The great hall would be modelled on those of the royal villas he was familiar with and it might well be impossible for a modern archaeologist to distinguish his villa buildings from those of his royal lord. So was the western complex of halls at Cowdery's Down built for a noble warrior granted an estate for a single life? It would explain the seeming contradiction of its grandeur combined with the short-term nature of its existence (33).

The Christian Church broke the principles of landholding on which this system was based. Individual priests, abbots or bishops will surely die, but the Church as a corporate organization will survive for ever, or at least until the Day

32 *Reconstruction of Cowdery's Down Hall C12, which illustrates the quantity of oak required in the construction of a great hall, particularly if it had a suspended plank floor. Perhaps this hall was built for a nobleman who had been granted an estate by the king which returned to the royal estate on his death.*

of Judgement. Its claim to ownership of land once given was tenacious and it was the Church which in the seventh century introduced the practice of recording in writing all gifts of land to it. Noblemen and women wishing to grant land to found monasteries or add to the estates

51

33 *Alternative reconstructions for the exterior appearance of Cowdery's Down Hall C12 illustrate how little we still know about the roofs of excavated timber buildings. The 'Old English thatched cottage' version (right) would be functional, if a little dull, but we can borrow some elements from Norwegian stave churches and put wooden shingles on its roof to make it much more dramatic (above).*

of existing monasteries needed the king's permission to alienate land in this way and these grants were also recorded in writing. From there it was but a short step for grants from the king to laymen being written down rather than made verbally in public before witnesses: a thoroughly appropriate process for a short-term grant of land. The final stage saw noble-men request that the land grants to them become permanent, to be passed on to their successors on an hereditary basis, alienating these estates from royal ownership.

So while some settlements containing halls the same size as that at Yeavering may indeed be royal estate centres, many others may have been constructed for noblemen or else belonged to abbots and bishops, for instance North-ampton. Any documents which might have recorded such land grants have usually long since perished. Still, if it is not possible to be sure precisely who owned any particular settlement, we can at least use their large timber buildings as a measure of the resources controlled by landowners. We can also relate the activities which took place in them to Bede's descriptions and the *Beowulf* poem. Great halls such as Yeavering A4 would have had crossbeams high enough to suspend a chain and cooking cauldron nearly 3m (10ft) above the hearth. This is the length of the chain and cauldron found in the Sutton Hoo ship burial. The raised plank platforms of Hall A4 would have carried the feasting tables at which heroic poems would be recited to the accompaniment of much eating and drinking.

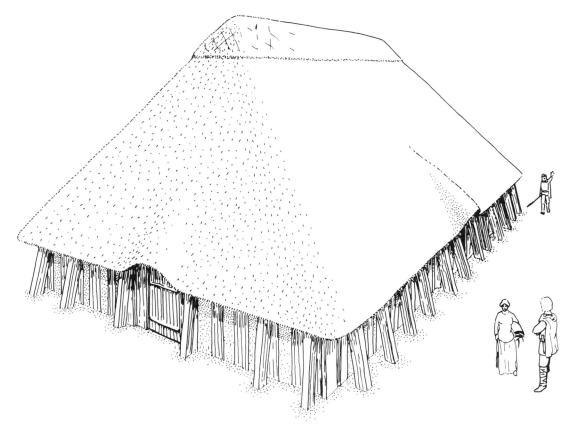

5

Burial practices and structures

At first glance, the study of ancient communities through their dead may seem a macabre, rather ghoulish activity. But if we are to discover more about the people who occupied the hamlets and farmsteads we have uncovered, we must take advantage of the rich evidence of the excavated burial grounds of this period (34). In the past, understanding of Anglo-Saxon cemeteries has been dominated by the study of the objects which accompanied so many of the burials, notably brooches, buckles and other dress fittings, various types of containers, everyday tools such as knives and keys, and also iron weapons. Yet these represent only part of the story, for where there is a combination of good preservation of evidence with careful excavation and recording, we can recover valuable information about the actual process of burial and some aspects of the ritual associated with it.

Skeletal remains
Through the study of human bone and teeth we can calculate sex, stature and build, age at death and diet, as well as detect accidents such as broken bones, the effects of diseases suffered and other medical conditions such as arthritis. Evidence for nutritional deficiencies, particularly in childhood when growth can be stunted, are detectable. The wear patterns and presence or lack of decay on teeth can tell us a great deal about what people ate. The cemetery at Worthy Park near Winchester (Hampshire) has produced a number of spectacular case studies: a mother who died in childbirth, with the leg bones of her baby still trapped in her pelvis (Grave 26); a man of around 30 years, who had been born without his left upper limb (Grave 38); and rather less certainly a violent rape of

a sixteen-year old girl, diagnosed from evidence for a muscle tear on her right thigh (Grave 78), though some experts believe that this tear might have had a more innocent explanation. Blood groupings and DNA characteristics may also be established in the future from such material, though they do not yet feature in cemetery reports in England. Other aspects of the bone evidence (called non-metrical traits) may reveal family relationships within a community, though how they should be interpreted remains controversial.

Indeed we should be aware that there are real problems in assessing this type of evidence. Certain key parts of the skeleton are necessary to ascertain sex accurately. When the complete skeleton is available for study in good condition, a situation which depends largely on the acidity of the surrounding soil, the degree of accuracy for sexing can be more than 90 per cent. But in many excavated cemeteries bone preservation is distinctly variable and accurate sexing is rather more difficult to achieve.

Cemeteries in acid sand or gravel soils yield little or no bone; tooth enamel is the last element to survive in such circumstances. Sometimes there is no visible trace of a corpse, though chemical residues can be detected in the soil. In other cases, fine dark soil filters downwards with percolating rainwater through the coarser soil of the grave fill and gradually replaces both flesh and bone as it breaks down. This leaves a soil shadow which can be excavated and recorded, as at Mucking, or from which three-dimensional casts can be made as at Sutton Hoo.

Age is particularly difficult to estimate once an individual achieves maturity at around 21 years and past estimates for adults can be badly

34 *Map showing principal sites discussed in chapters 5–7.*

wrong. Analysis of datable eighteenth- and nineteenth-century burials from the crypts at Spitalfields Church in London demonstrated the problem when conventional methods of estimating ages were applied to them. As a result of this, a tendency to understate the true age at death must be allowed for now. It is also difficult to compare the results from different cemeteries, when they have been studied by various specialists over a wide period of time, each using their own set of criteria to reach their conclusions about age. Again the tables

for estimating stature from the dimensions of the long bones of the legs and arms have changed over the years. It would seem that all the skeletal material from the older excavation reports will need to be reassessed before it can be compared to that obtained from recently-published sites.

Burial practices
Many of the dead were cremated and a selection of the burnt bone usually placed in some kind of container normally referred to as an urn,

most commonly of pottery though bronze vessels also occur. This container was then buried in a pit either individually or in a cluster (**colour plates 2-3**). Sometimes settings of stones have been found marking these pits. Other individuals were buried unburnt in deep rectangular pits or graves: this is inhumation. Both types of burial can occur in the same cemetery and it seems that members of the community had a choice. As the cemeteries of the continental homelands in north Germany and southern Scandinavia also contain both burial practices, it was a choice that they brought with them.

On the other hand, Late Roman burial practice in Britain and throughout the Western Roman Empire was almost exclusively inhumation, with cremation going out of fashion during the third century AD. Perhaps individuals in Anglo-Saxon communities could indicate in their lifetime how they wished to be buried, trusting their relations to honour their request, much as we do today. Alternatively the decision may have rested with the head of the family clan, whose views would be dominant on such issues.

It is difficult to know also whether allegiance to a particular god or goddess or family of gods was crucial in deciding the form of the burial. Perhaps as the flames and smoke ascended during the process of cremation, the spirit or soul of the individual was seen as being freed from the body and was sent on its journey to an afterlife. Equally, the unburnt fully-dressed corpse in a grave seems to be equipped so that the deceased might be recognized in the other world for what he or she had been in life.

Although our written sources belong to a later period, it might be supposed that a great warrior could expect to be welcomed at Valhalla to feast and swap yarns with his ancestors and contemporaries, but also to serve Wodan in battle against the Giants or other enemies. Certainly virtually every Anglo-Saxon royal genealogy of the seventh, eighth and ninth centuries claimed Wodan as an ancestor. For this purpose, it would be important for him to be buried with weapons and armour, as in the famous Sutton Hoo ship burial, so that there would be no doubt about his place in the hall of the gods.

Much is still unknown about the pagan religious beliefs of the Anglo-Saxons. Inscriptions in runic letters and religious symbols on objects such as cremation pottery containers confirm their paganism. Most of our information, however, comes from early Roman accounts, notably by Tacitus who wrote at the end of the first century AD about the Germans of northern Europe, or else from late medieval Scandinavian literature, mostly from christianized Iceland. Some archaeologists argue that the role of religious belief and ritual in determining the form of burial practice was very important. Others are more sceptical and would see social conformity and traditionalism as having more significance in this matter.

Inhumation burial

Let us first try to reconstruct a typical inhumation burial, using the range of evidence available to archaeologists. The grave itself was not always dug to the correct size to fit the individual who was actually placed in it (**35**). There are graves which are too large, but, perhaps more significantly, quite a number which are too short, with the body stuffed in, sometimes rather unceremoniously. This implies that the grave was excavated in advance of the burial, perhaps during the time when the dying individual or the recently-deceased corpse was lying some distance away, perhaps in the settlement. It may even be the case that a number of graves were dug each year, while the ground was still soft and before winter set in. They would be left covered over until needed and then they would be quickly cleaned out and prepared. This would help to explain the occasional presence of empty graves, which seem never to have contained a burial, and which can occur even in cemeteries where bone preservation was good.

Some burials may have been placed directly into an unlined grave, but some kind of wooden or stone lining occurs quite often. The version in wood is often referred to as a 'coffin' (**36**). If by a coffin is meant a wooden box in which the corpse already lay, prior to the box being lowered into the grave, then in most cases it is an inappropriate term. What is found instead are traces of wooden planks placed down the sides of the grave with soil, or soil and stones, packed between the planks and the edge of the grave cut. The body was then lowered into the enclosed area, presumably using ropes. Sometimes a stone or other object was placed to act as a sort of pillow below the head, and a plank or planks were laid down as a cover

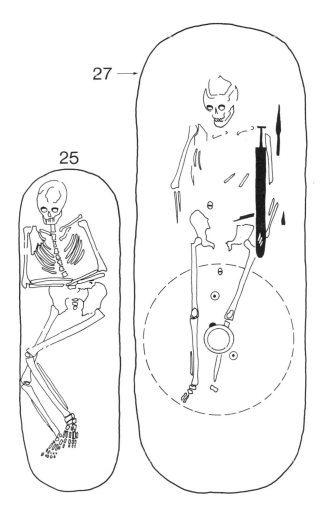

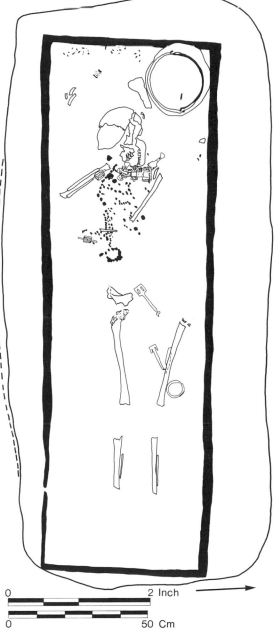

35 *Plans of two seventh-century inhumation burials at Buckland, Dover (Kent): the adult woman in Grave 25 is squeezed into her grave with her legs flexed, while the man extended on his back in Grave 27 occupies a much larger burial pit and was accompanied by a sword, spear and shield.*

over the corpse before the grave was backfilled.

This results in a very loose fill with large numbers of voids in the lower part of the grave immediately above the skeleton. As the wooden planking above the corpse rots and the body decomposes, so the soil from above gradually subsides to surround the bone. On occasion an object, such as a shield, has clearly been placed above the upper planks and as those planks and the thin wooden boards of the shield disintegrate, its iron boss and handle eventually

36 *Plan of Sewerby (Humberside) Grave 49 with the clear soil stain of four 'coffin' planks enclosing a relatively rich young woman's extended burial. Datable within the sixth century, she had a bronze bowl placed above her head and wore clothing fastened by brooches with beads strung between them. Clasps fastened her sleeves at the wrist and two imitation keys called girdle hangers were suspended from her waist.*

collapse down into the void between the upper planks and the corpse, often ending up at a rather strange angle of rest. Sometimes the wooden structure is enclosed by individual large stones and more such stones can also be placed over the upper planks (**37** and **38**). All this would leave quite a large amount of surplus soil, which could not be backfilled into the grave, but might well be piled instead over the grave in a low mound which marked its position for a time.

37 & 38 *Two views of Lechlade (Glos.) Grave 18, showing the reuse of Roman building stone from a local villa to fill the upper part of the grave and the richly dressed woman buried here in the sixth century within traces of a wooden 'coffin' wearing brooches and beads below her chin and accompanied by many other dress-fittings.*

Much larger wooden-lined graves are sometimes found and these are referred to as chamber graves. These are noticeably deeper, broader and longer than the simple 'coffin'-type burials. Sometimes the body seems to have been placed in a separate wooden 'coffin', but in others the corpse was simply laid out within the chamber. Rarer still are burials in boats, whether within a simple dug-out canoe as recently excavated at Snape (Suffolk) (**39**), or an elaborate planked vessel of clinker-construction, as in the famous Sutton Hoo mound 1 ship burial (see pp. 91–2). The latter had its burial deposit in a special wooden house or roofed chamber constructed amidships within the boat, while in mound 2 the body lay in a rectangular wooden chamber 3.8 by 1.5m (12 by 5ft) with a clinker-built boat placed over it and a mound over that. Such elaborate chamber-grave structures involve much investment of labour and materials and are attributed to the wealthiest and most powerful families of Anglo-Saxon society. Their burial grounds seem to be

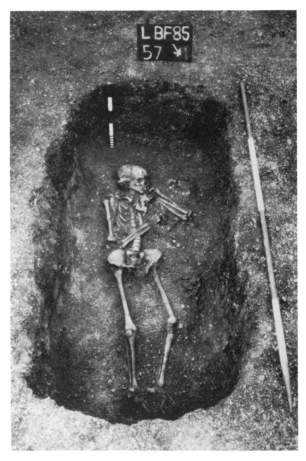

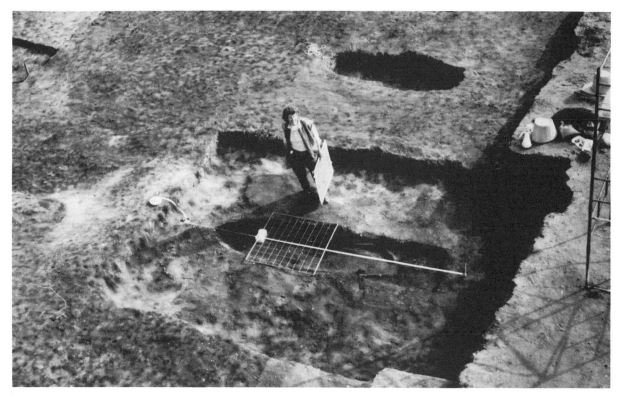

the equivalents of the settlements with great halls and like them they make their first appearance in the later sixth and early seventh centuries.

Shelves along the sides of graves and notches dug into the upper sections of the grave sides presumably belong to other wooden grave structures. Whether these represent cross-beams for structures within the upper part of the grave, or foundation posts for a canopy or house-like structure over the grave cannot at present be decided. A number of such structures are known from cemeteries in Kent where the graves were dug into the chalk bedrock, preserving clear traces of these internal shelves and notches. The cemetery at St Peter's, Broad-stairs, was the first of these Kentish sites to be discussed in detail (40).

Other features found at this site included post-holes at each corner, implying a canopy structure over the grave, and annular (complete ring) and penannular (broken ring) ditches, which might have marked the edge of the low mounds over the graves or contained a wooden fence around the mound, as might the narrow rectangular slots found there. Post-holes for posts or even 'totem-poles' acting as markers

39 *A view of a dug-out canoe in a grave at Snape (Suffolk) covering an inhumation burial accompanied by a pair of drinking horns. Probably datable to the sixth century on the basis of objects from neighbouring graves. Similar canoe burials are known from the Baltic island of Bornholm (Denmark), but have never previously been recognized in England.*

occurred adjacent to graves and in the short gap between the ends of some of the penannular ditches (41). We can only guess whether such posts were carved or painted and whether they bore inscriptions in the runic alphabet, for none have survived intact, but it would be surprising if they had not been marked in some way.

Body positions
The position of the corpse in the grave is normally supine, that is it has been laid extended on its back with the legs straight or slightly flexed. The arms would either be by

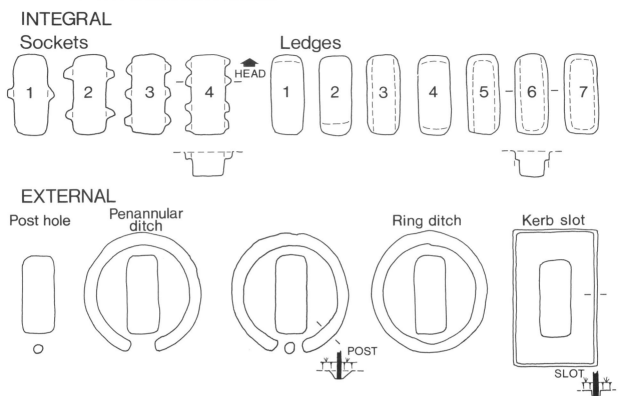

40 *Grave structures recovered in the chalk bedrock of the seventh-century cemetery excavated at St Peter's, Broadstairs (Kent). Sockets take crossbeams and possibly also support a wooden canopy above the grave; ledges possibly have a similar function; features external to the grave, annular and penannular ring-ditches and rectangular kerb-slots, may contain a light fence around the grave or enclose a low mound over the grave, while post-holes imply a marker post or totem pole by the grave.*

the side, or else the lower arms were placed across the body, or perhaps one or both hands were left resting over the waist or pelvis. More unusual positions include the body being laid on its side in a crouching posture, though the back may be left straight with the legs pulled up, rather than being in the true crouched position. In this, the back was curved with the legs drawn up in a near-foetal position. It has been argued that as the crouched position is found in pre-Roman and Roman burials in

Britain, its presence may indicate a British burial practice and a mixed British and Anglo-Saxon population.

Much more research still needs to be carried out on this question before an answer can be proposed. It raises the whole question of whether it is possible to distinguish between the Anglo-Saxon incomers and the native British population from the skeletal evidence. As both populations belong to a common, genetically-mixed stock occupying northern Europe, it may not be feasible. On the other hand, many of the weapon burials in early cemeteries belong to well-built, strong men either side of six foot in height and the accompanying women are often near or only slightly below modern heights. It is tempting to contrast these individuals with the slighter-built skeletons recovered from Late Roman cemeteries in Britain and label them as Anglo-Saxon immigrants. Future work on

41 *Plan of the St Peter's, Broadstairs, cemetery. A significant proportion of graves were accompanied by sockets, ledges, ring-ditches or kerb-slots.*

blood-typing and DNA analysis may take us further, but for now the evidence is rather unsatisfactory.

There is also the relatively rare practice of prone burial, burying the individual face-down. This too is a practice we can find in Late Roman cemeteries in Britain. It is often seen as a form of punishment to be equated perhaps with the practice of decapitation. This need not mean that all or even a majority of the prone burials recovered were actually buried alive, but a few may have been. Similarly decapitation need not have been the cause of death, particularly as the cut was sometimes administered from the front. Rather we seem to be seeing a practice of post-mortem removal of the head, which was sometimes placed separately in the grave and at other times was disposed of in some other way.

Ritual decapitation might be an attempt to prevent the spirit of a powerful and feared individual from haunting the living. Attempts to explain a prone burial placed above a conventional supine burial as the ritual killing of a wife after the death of her husband (the *suttee* theory) fall down when it is clear that it is not always a woman buried above a man. Nor is it the sacrifice of a slave to their master or mistress. In a case from the Sewerby cemetery near the Yorkshire coast, a richly-dressed young woman was buried in a deep grave below the prone burial of an older woman, respectably dressed with brooches and other fittings. Yet a single and relatively light stone had been placed over the middle of her back and her limbs were distorted, as if she had been buried alive. The suggestion that she was being punished because she was considered to have caused the death of the young lady, perhaps by poison or witchcraft, is a real possibility. Not everyone is convinced that live burial was practised, but it has been suggested that prone burial and decapitation were alternative punishments for witches and warlocks, whether as a form of execution or as penalties exacted after death.

Dress fittings
Metal dress fittings in graves also provide information about burial practices. The corrosion products of brooches often preserve in mineral form an impression of the textiles they fastened and even on occasion actual fragments of the organic threads themselves. Thus they demonstrate that individuals were normally buried fully dressed, though whether in their everyday dress or in an equivalent to a best suit or favourite dress today is a matter of debate. The same metal corrosion products can also sometimes preserve the pupal cases of insects such as blow-flys. Where these are present, they demonstrate that a delay of several days elapsed between death and burial, during which the corpse played host to these insects.

Regional female dress fashions can be detected from the late fifth century for a hundred years or more, perhaps indicating a recognizable sixth-century folk costume (**42**). In the provinces attributed by Bede to the Saxons (Sussex, Wessex, Surrey, west Kent, Essex and the south Midlands), the finest-dressed women had a pair of brooches on or near the collar bones to fasten the top edge of a tubular cloth dress (called a *peplos* costume) either side of the shoulders, with a string or strings of beads attached to each brooch's pin fittings. A third brooch worn centrally over the chest may have been used to fasten the tubular dress to a tailored undergarment with or without loose sleeves. An alternative function would be to fasten a light cloak, head-scarf or veil over the main dress, which was also held in place at the waist by a belt, usually fastened with a metal buckle. A bag containing trinkets, or a set of simple keys, a string of beads, or perhaps an iron firesteel might be hanging from such a belt and a domestic knife might be placed either near her lower arm (perhaps in a cloth sheath sewn onto a sleeve) or near the waist belt.

The well-dressed woman in the Anglian regions (east Midlands, East Anglia, Lincolnshire, Yorkshire, Northumberland and

42 *Three women dressed in regional fashions of the sixth century: (*Left*) the* Anglian *undergarment has long tailored sleeves fastened at the wrist by metal clasps; (*Right*) the* Saxon *undergarment is sleeveless or has loose sleeves; (*Centre*) the* Kentish *woman wears a skirt under a tailored jacket or coat fastened at the front by small brooches linked by a short chain below the neck and two larger brooches below the waist, while suspended from her waist was a spoon and a rock crystal ball set in a metal sling. (Peter Dunn.)*

Durham) would be similarly dressed, except that the range of brooches was somewhat different and the undergarment had long tailored sleeves fastened by cuff-link-like fittings called wrist clasps. These small hook-and-eye metal fittings were sewn on to either side of a split sleeve and are extremely rare in England outside this region. Keys and mock keys called girdle hangers also play a prominent role in Anglian dress, perhaps reflecting the role of well-born women as keepers of the family wealth and therefore the holders of keys to boxes and chests. The wealthiest might also wear decorated silver bracelets on one or both of their arms or else a silver neck ring.

Kent, east of the river Medway, together with the Isle of Wight were provinces of the Jutes, open to continental fashions from their Frankish neighbours and possible overlords in the sixth and seventh centuries. Fine silver (later gold) brooches inlaid with semi-precious garnet stones, glass and paste-and-shell settings were worn in similar positions to those of women found in Frankish cemeteries. Rock crystal balls suspended from the waist in silver band settings and cloth bands braided with gold thread around the head were also Frankish fashions.

A distinction should probably be drawn between those objects which are present as dress-fittings of a properly dressed corpse and others which were specifically added as grave goods to accompany the dead on their journey to the next world. The finding of nuts, fruit or eggs in a bowl, or the presence of other containers, associated with the consumption of alcoholic drinks, can be seen as the provision of food and drink to ease the journey of the dead. On the other hand, they might also indicate that the deceased had been a generous host in his or her lifetime. These vessels were normally placed at either the head or the foot end of the grave. Glass vessels, small pots, metal-bound stave buckets or small wooden bowls are commonly close to the skull. Larger vessels and wooden boxes and caskets are more often found below the feet.

Weapons in graves
The role of weapons, with the spear placed beside the body, its point above the head, the buckler-sized shield above the head, chest, waist or upper legs, and, where present, a sword or the short single-bladed seax parallel to the

body is more problematic. They are not strictly part of the dress and yet they are an extension of it. Detailed analysis by Heinrich Härke has demonstrated that the majority of weapon burials contain just a spear (44 per cent) or a spear and a shield (26 per cent). Contrary to first impressions, however, we find that relatively few of these graves contain full, functional working sets of weapons, such as would be required in battle. Rather individual weapons seem to be selected for inclusion in a grave from armouries inherited by the heirs of those commemorated in this way.

By no means all adolescent and adult male inhumation burials were accompanied by weapons. Quite apart from those individuals apparently buried without associated objects, a significant proportion of male burials entirely lacked any weapons. Instead they contained buckles and domestic knives and sometimes other fittings as well, such as iron firesteels or toilet implements. The full significance of this situation is not clear, but it should be noted that pagan priests were permitted neither to carry weapons nor ride stallions. According to Bede, a high priest at Edwin of Northumbria's court broke with paganism by mounting a stallion and casting a spear from horseback into a pagan enclosure at Goodmanham in Yorkshire, in order to desecrate it.

Finally it should be noted that occasionally charred wood or tree branches are found in the upper fills of graves. We do not know the correct explanation for this phenomenon, but fire rituals to cleanse the partially-backfilled grave, or the deliberate deposition of part of the fire used to prepare a grave-side meal might be possibilities. Of course this practice might also be linked to devotion to a god, such as Thor, associated with fire.

Cremation burial
It is surprising how much can be reconstructed of this practice, despite the obvious fire damage. The identification of the sex or age of individuals can be achieved providing certain crucial bone or teeth elements are present in a recognizable form, though the categories of age defined are broader than for well-preserved inhumed skeletons. The body seems to have been laid out fully dressed on the ground surface in a supine position (43), just as with an inhumation burial. A pyre or large bonfire was then constructed over the body, which

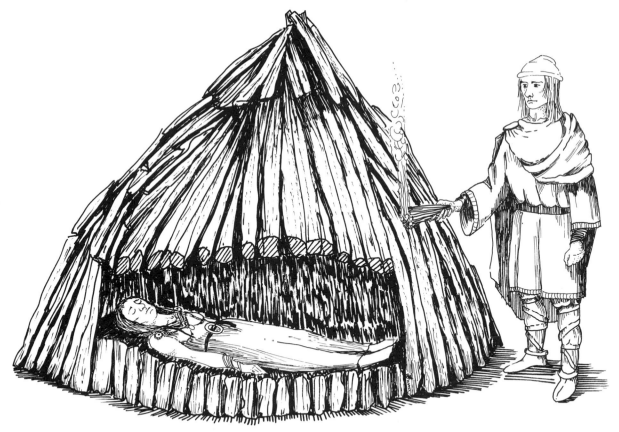

reached temperatures similar to those of a modern crematorium furnace, that is 900°C (1652°F). The temperature can be gauged by testing the heat at which glass beads, worn strung between pairs of brooches on the chest, begin to melt and fuse, matching those found in cremation urns. Body fats fuelled the burning process once the initial bonfire has achieved the correct temperature for a sufficient period of time (**44**).

Significantly the *scapulae* or shoulder blades are often not fully burnt in Anglo-Saxon cremations, in contrast to modern methods. This indicates that the corpse was lying flat on the natural land surface, since being in contact with the ground the shoulders were partially protected from the cremation process. This body position also explains the frequent presence of a light material found among the cremated bone and usually referred to as cremation slag or clinker. It is not a product of burning human hair, as was once thought, but appears to result from silica-bearing sandy soil under the body fusing with pyre material during the burning process.

43 *Reconstruction of a cremation pyre. The wife's body has been placed fully dressed in an extended position on the ground, as if in an inhumation grave and the pyre then constructed over her.*

The presence of pieces of glass vessel fused to fragments of skull bone indicate that such vessels were placed by the head, just as they would have been for an inhumation burial. Glass beads fused to long bones from the arms and from the chest area imply that the arms were crossed over the chest in such cases. Weapons are extremely rare and it seems probable that they were not normally laid out around or over the body, in contrast to inhumation burials.

Analysis of the cremated bone recovered from urns indicates that only selected bones were deposited in this formal way. Usually these came from the head and chest area, together with some of the long bones. They seem to have been placed initially in cloth bags, as separate

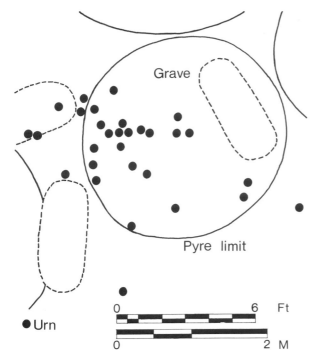

44 *Plan of the dark greasy stain left by an excavated cremation pyre in the Liebenau (Germany) cemetery. An inhumation grave dug through the pyre at a later date was big enough to take a corpse and provides a human scale for the area, 3m (10ft) in diameter, covered by this pyre.*

groups of bone are visible within pots. Sometimes the bones in a cloth bag were buried directly into a prepared hole. These are the so-called unurned cremations. Wooden bowls may also have been used as containers, though none has ever been recognized, but bronze bowls seem to represent the upper-class container for cremation burials, as at Coombe in Kent and several mounds at Sutton Hoo.

Unburnt objects of metal, antler or bone are a peculiar feature of cremation deposits. In a few cases particular objects may have accidently escaped burning or heat distortion from the pyre, but some are deliberately added token objects. Toilet implements such as pairs of tweezers, razors and combs frequently appear as tiny miniatures, which have a symbolic rather than a functional role. They are funerary substitutes for the real thing. In view of the role of such toilet implements in the present-ation and shaving of hair, as well as moustaches and beards and the emphasis on selecting cremated bone from the skull and upper body for the urn, it is tempting to see a connection. Was the head considered the most important element of the body, and the one in which the spirit resided?

Contamination of the bones from the main individual represented in an urn with a few from one or more others of a different age or sex may reflect the reuse or the overlapping of pyres. Or it might instead represent a deliberate practice of adding 'token' bones of a relative or friend. The presence of cremated animal bones also needs some explanation. Are they part of the funeral feast added to the pyre or were whole animals or parts of them sacrificed and then added to the pyre assemblage? They include both domesticated breeds such as pig, sheep, cattle and horse, dogs and cats, as well as wild creatures such as red and roe deer and water fowl. The occasional and very rare inhumation burial of dog or horse among other inhumation burials should also be noted, though it is much more common in the continental homelands of the Anglo-Saxons.

Cremation burial structures

Small ring-ditches which were sometimes constructed around a central cremation pit (with or without an urn) may imply a mound over the burial deposit, as with inhumation burials. Larger mounds are associated with the more elaborate cremations in bronze vessels from Sutton Hoo, which also include unburnt objects. There are also post-hole structures around and above cremations, which imply miniature wooden 'houses of the dead' to commemorate cremation deposits (**45**). These have been identified now at several Anglo-Saxon cemeteries in southern England from the late fifth century onwards, notably at Apple Down in West Sussex (**46**). They were quite common in Roman-period and much later cemeteries in the Netherlands and north-west Germany, where cremation was still being practised in the eighth century (**47**).

Cremation pyres at Liebenau and Sancton

We have to turn to the Saxon homelands, and in particular to the remarkably well-preserved evidence from the Liebenau cemetery, to see

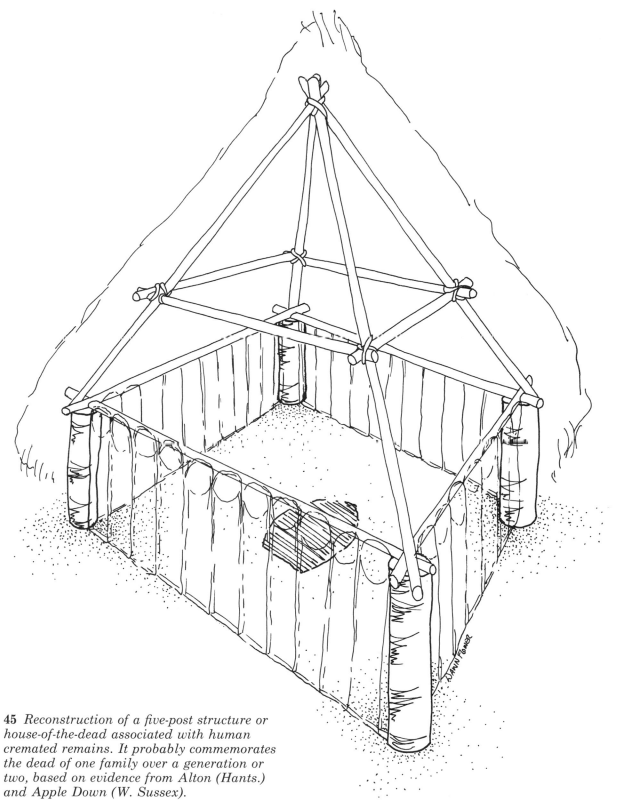

45 *Reconstruction of a five-post structure or house-of-the-dead associated with human cremated remains. It probably commemorates the dead of one family over a generation or two, based on evidence from Alton (Hants.) and Apple Down (W. Sussex).*

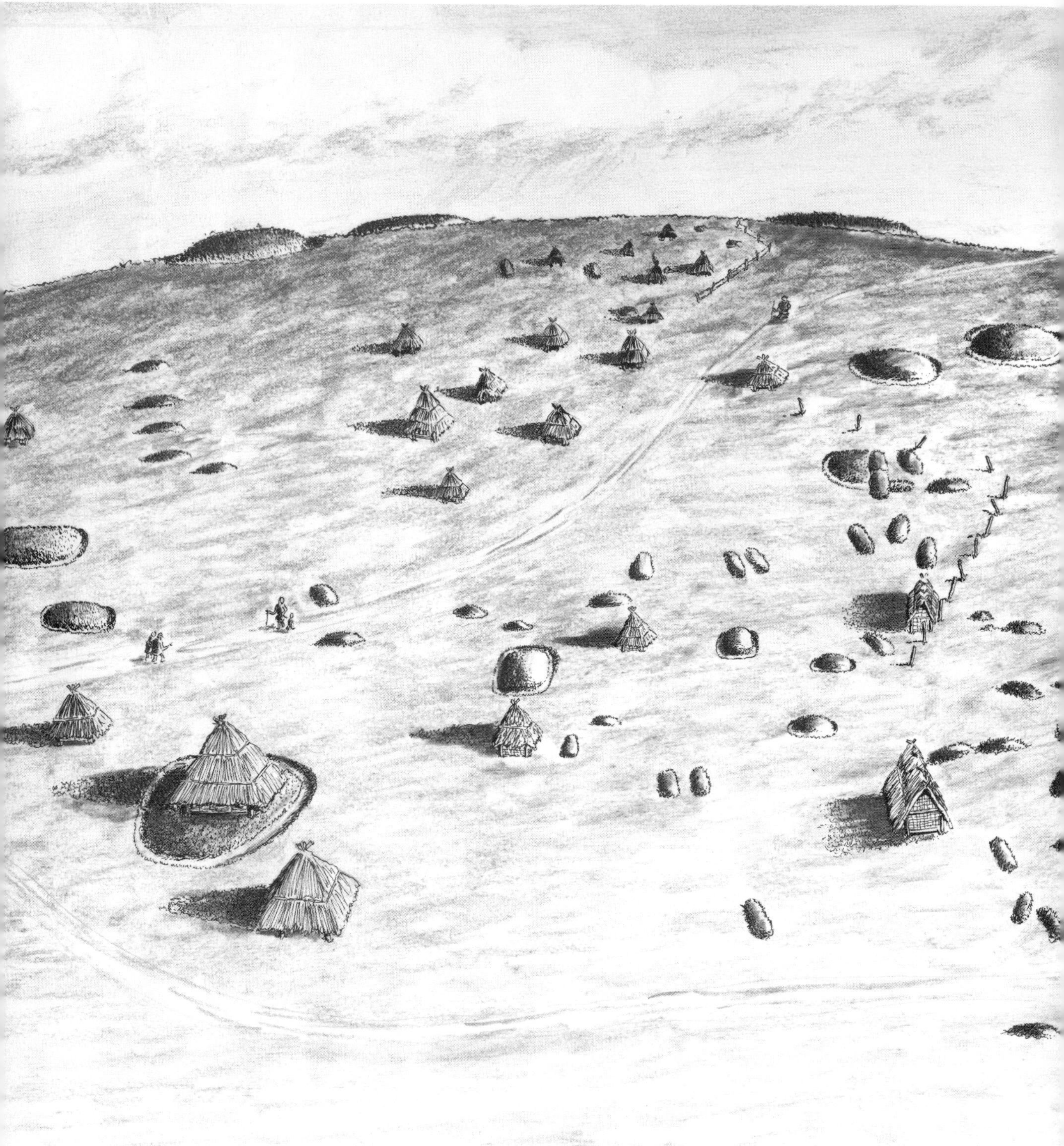

what archaeological remains can be left from the cremation pyres of this period (see **44**). Each pyre there was a burnt oval or circular area of between 3m (10ft) and 4·5m (15ft). Complete pots containing cremated remains were buried within the pyre area, but other fragments of burnt pot seem to indicate that pottery vessels were ritually broken and thrown on to the pyre before or during the cremation. Post-holes showing evidence for burning in them may form part of the pyre structure, but others may represent site markers, and stones also seem to have been used sometimes to mark the position of pyres and cremation depositions. Part of such a pyre area has been tentatively identified within the excavated cremation cemetery of Sancton in the Yorkshire Wolds and others may yet be recognized where they have escaped modern plough-damage. As such evidence was never deeply buried, it requires extremely good fortune to find pyre remains in a relatively undisturbed state.

So to conclude, cremation and inhumation burial practices share more in common than we might at first expect. The position in which the corpse was laid out is the same, whether it was within the confines of a grave or on the ground surface before the pyre was constructed. In either case the body was normally deposited fully dressed and, where this was considered appropriate, it might be accompanied by vessels of glass, pottery or wood, placed either by the head or at the foot of the grave. Weapons only accompanied a cremation burial in the most exceptional circumstances in England, but were much more common among inhumation burials. Similarly miniature toilet implements and combs were limited to cremation deposits and are never found with inhumation burials, though these might on occasion contain full-

46 *Reconstruction of Apple Down Cemetery 1 datable from the late fifth to the seventh century. Each inhumation grave was probably marked by a small earth mound or occasionally by posts, while some cremations were marked by small timber houses-of-the-dead or by ring-ditches enclosing low mounds. (Chichester District Archaeology Unit.)*

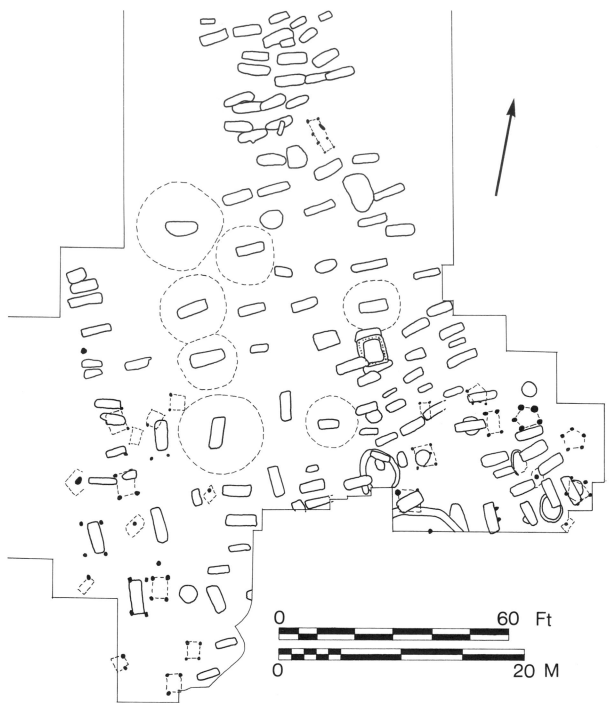

47 *Plan of the seventh- to eighth-century cemetery at Oldendorf near Lüneburg (Germany) containing four-post and five-post cremation structures similar to those found at Apple Down and other Anglo-Saxon cemeteries as well as inhumation graves.*

sized toilet implements or combs. This reflects both the importance of these implements in cremation practices and the need to make provision against the destructiveness of the flames by including unburnt symbolic miniatures of objects.

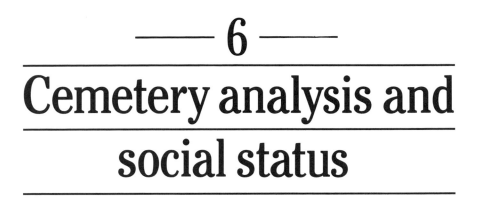

6

Cemetery analysis and social status

The distribution of burial practices

Although both cremation and inhumation burial often occur in the same cemetery, there are regional and chronological patterns in which one or other burial rite is dominant. Broadly speaking, cemeteries with large numbers of cremations in pottery urns are relatively rare south of the Thames valley. Cremation urnfields with several thousand pots are restricted to East Anglia, the east Midlands and southeast Yorkshire, for instance Lackford (Suffolk), Spong Hill (Norfolk), Newark (Nottinghamshire), Cleatham and Sancton (Humberside, formerly Lincolnshire and East Riding of Yorkshire respectively)

These are the English counterparts of even larger urnfields in north Germany and south Scandinavia, the homelands of the Saxons and Angles. Examples are Westerwanna and Issendorf in Lower Saxony and Bordesholm and Süderbrarup further north in Schleswig-Holstein. Thames valley cemeteries, such as that excavated at Abingdon near Oxford in the 1930s, with roughly half of its burials deposited as cremations, have been seen as marking a boundary zone between the two burial practices. In the regions south of the Thames inhumation predominated, so the traditional view went, whereas north of that river cremation was the leading rite.

This turns out to be an over-simplification of a rather more complicated situation. Excavations of three cemeteries in Hampshire since the 1960s and another more recently in West Sussex suggest that cremation burial may have been significantly underestimated as a result of poor excavation technique in the past. Although many of the cremations found at Alton, Andover and Worthy Park (Hampshire) and Apple Down (West Sussex) were deposited in pottery urns, others came from unurned contexts, which require rather more care and skill successfully to locate and excavate.

Deposits of cremated bone accompanied by burnt or heat-distorted metal or glass objects collected in a cloth bag and then deposited directly into a pit are readily disturbed by modern ploughing and are easy to overlook. Further modern excavation of cemeteries in East Sussex, Berkshire, Surrey and Kent is needed before we can seriously assess the relative importance of cremation burial south of the Thames between the fifth and seventh centuries. Old excavations provide sufficient evidence to indicate that some cremation in pottery urns took place within Jutish Kent in the fifth century, but it is not clear to what extent this burial practice continued there into the sixth century.

If cremation south of the Thames needs reassessing, then so does inhumation in the Anglian provinces of East Anglia, the east Midlands, Lincolnshire and Yorkshire. Relatively small cemeteries of inhumation graves represent population sizes which seem to match those estimated for small hamlet settlements of the West Stow or Chalton type. These burial grounds are scattered across the landscape and are far more numerous than the larger cremation cemeteries which have attracted so much attention. The majority of these inhumation cemeteries can be dated to the sixth century, some with origins back in the later fifth and some probably continuing on into the early seventh century.

The partially investigated cemetery on the Yorkshire Wolds at Sewerby or the almost completely excavated site by Norton-on-Tees in Cleveland are more typical of sixth-century burial grounds in north-east England than the three cremation urnfields at Sancton and at The Mount and Heworth beside York. Attached to one corner of the Spong Hill cremation cemetery is another such inhumation grave field representing a small sixth-century community. It buried its 58 dead separately from its cremating neighbours, though in an adjacent area. Whether the Spong Hill settlements were similarly distinct is one of the many interesting questions which we can only begin to answer with further excavation of the settlement complex surrounding this burial ground.

The purpose of cemetery analysis

Cemetery analysis is undertaken with the aim of firstly establishing the sequence of development of the burial ground and its organization, in order to provide an estimate for the size of the community it represents in any particular generation. It then goes on to attempt to assess the relative status within that community of the individuals buried in each generation. Obviously much more information can be obtained from well-furnished inhumation burials than from cremation deposits, though it is surprising how much we can learn from analysis of an urnfield.

Ideally a cemetery that has been as fully excavated as possible should be used, so that it closely represents a near-complete community in death. It is not always easy to establish the original extent of a cemetery. Boundary ditches or other linear markers which might be equivalent to the brick or stone walls enclosing a modern cemetery or churchyard are not a common feature of Early Anglo-Saxon cemeteries. Also part of the cemetery may already have been destroyed by road-building or quarrying, which unfortunately are the usual means by which the existence of these burial grounds is discovered.

It is rare indeed that burial sites are located through such means as air photography, as at Updown near Eastry (Kent) (48). Even in that particular case, although many individual graves and ring-ditches which enclose some of the burials are clearly visible, the graves stop suddenly along a straight line two-thirds of the way across the field. This is the result of a change of crop grown on the field to one less sensitive to the presence of the graves. The second crop conceals a continuation of this

cemetery eastwards beside and under the present woodland, which was only revealed during a small-scale excavation in advance of a gas pipeline being laid across the field.

High standards of excavation and a full and accurate record of each grave would ideally be matched by good preservation of human bone, so that the results of a human biologist's studies can be added to the range of archaeological data. Nevertheless, much can still be achieved with cemeteries which lack any form of bone preservation, or contain little more than soil silhouettes, providing there is an accurate record of the positioning of the various items in the grave.

Social status

The relative status of any individual burial can be established from two sets of data. First there is the amount of effort and care which has been expended on the construction of the grave itself. The deeper, the longer and the wider it is, the more effort was required in terms of man-hours in digging. Equally the quantity of timber used to construct a 'coffin' or chamber is again an indication of relative importance, as is any above-ground structure such as a burial mound, which could take up a significantly larger area than that given over to lesser 'coffin' burials.

Secondly the elaborateness of the dress fastenings and the range of other objects buried with each individual can be taken as an indication of their relative rank within the community and possibly indeed within other communities in the immediate vicinity and beyond. Certainly we can successfully create on paper, in the form of charts or diagrams, hierarchies of the range of objects buried with men, women and even children within these cemeteries. The difficult thing is to decide what these hierarchies actually represented in the real

48 (Above) An air photo of the seventh-century cemetery at Updown, Eastry (Kent). Note the way it seems to stop along a straight line within the field. Some crops are less sensitive to graves and ring-ditches and a change of crop demonstrates that here. (Cambridge University: copyright reserved.)

49 (Below) A view of the cemetery at Lechlade (Glos.) with the excavated graves clearly visible datable to both the sixth and seventh centuries.

world, in terms of relationships within particular communities. Are the objects buried with the dead entirely their personal possessions, or do they include items from a family-owned wardrobe and armoury? This is a question we will return to consider further.

Grave orientation

Grave orientation has often been seen as potentially significant and the precise alignments of grave cuts to the points of the compass are recorded with some care in a modern excavation (**49**). The majority are orientated W-E, with the head deposited at the west end, but there are entire cemeteries in which all the burials are aligned N-S or S-N with the head at the south end. There are also quite a few cemeteries in which both orientations seem to occur in equal numbers, for example at Apple Down. Because N-S burial occurs in north German cemeteries, this custom has been attributed to Anglo-Saxon immigrants, but a combination of N-S orientation and crouched burial can be found in Roman-period and even pre-Roman burials in northern Britain and has been seen as evidence for continuity of native British burial rites.

Nor can we simply assign all E-W burials to Christians, for this orientation seems to have been widely used in Anglo-Saxon pagan period cemeteries, long before the first Christian mission of Augustine in 597. Admittedly, some Anglo-Saxon cemeteries founded in the mid- and later seventh century seem to have been replacements for burial grounds which had pagan associations, as at Winnall near Winchester (Hampshire). They are characterized by regular rows of E-W graves and match the layout of (nominally Christian) Frankish cemeteries across the English Channel from the early sixth century to the early eighth century (the so-called row-grave cemeteries). On the other hand, it seems that E-W burial was the normal Late Roman inhumation practice, though cemeteries of native Gallo-Romans with N-S burial are also known in Late Roman Gaul.

We do not know precisely when Christian communities in western Europe adopted E-W inhumation as their exclusive mode of burial, but there is a suspicion that it only became official policy at a relatively late date. Study of the decisions of church councils reveals a distinct lack of interest by the Church in burial practice much before the eighth century AD. It

may well be that a Christian rationale was subsequently created for the adoption of the dominant form of Roman and post-Roman grave orientation. Fortunately this alignment matches that of a church, the altar of which was placed at the east end with its main entrance to the west.

It is time to turn to a particular example: the cemetery excavated by Sonia Hawkes near Finglesham (Kent). Here a study of grave orientation shows that the rather small (and presumably pagan) community buried here in the sixth century had their E-W graves aligned distinctly more towards the north than the subsequent (and presumably Christian) seventh-century graves. It was suggested that it might be possible to tell from this at which time of year a grave was dug. The theory was based on a belief that the grave diggers would be standing in the burial ground just before dawn and would align the outline of the grave cut to the sun as it rose over the horizon. Charts showing the changing angle of the sunrise within the solar arc through the year make a choice of two possible months during which any particular grave might be dug (**50**). This might enable us in turn to comment on the months at which members of a particular community were more likely to die and speculate on what led to a higher mortality rate at certain times of the year.

Burials can occur outside the solar arc, however, as is the case for most of the sixth-century graves at Finglesham (**51**). Another possible complicating factor would be the presence of higher ground around a cemetery, which would mean that sunrise would occur a little later and at a slightly different angle from the situation on level ground at or just above sea level. This was not a problem at Finglesham, whose burials were situated just over 30m (100ft) above modern sea level with a clear view of the English Channel to the east. More significantly records of seventeenth-century mortality rates seem to suggest that members of later rural communities died at a fairly even rate throughout the year. They do not show the pronounced peaks of death rates in late summer and early autumn or in late winter and early spring indicated by the solar arc chart at Finglesham. Surely there should be more deaths occurring in mid-winter, if the theory was correct. Alternatively it could be argued that graves were being dug each autumn before the ground

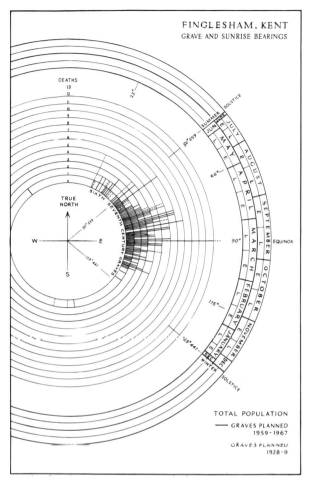

50 *Diagram relating the orientation of E-W graves of the sixth and seventh centuries at Finglesham (Kent) to the solar arc.*

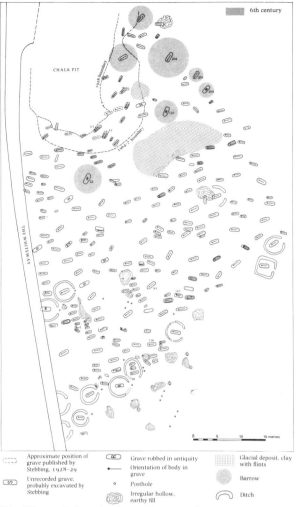

51 *Plan of the sixth- and seventh-century cemetery at Finglesham with shading over the potential areas of barrow mounds over individual graves.*

hardened, in anticipation of future deaths occurring through the winter.

While the first grave to be dug in a cemetery (or in a new sector of a burial ground) might be deliberately aligned to sunrise or sunset, subsequent graves could thereafter be orientated in relation to the low mound or some other marker of that initial burial and its neighbours. Also the influence of other local landmarks, which may or may not still be visible today, should not be ignored. It is not uncommon for prehistoric burial monuments to be incorporated into Anglo-Saxon cemeteries and to form a focus for the cemetery or a sector of it. This can be clearly seen in the recently-published cemetery plan of Buckland, Dover (Kent) in which a large barrow attracted a group of sixth-century burials (see **53** and **54**).

A fairly uniform orientation can occur, but many cemeteries have a mixture of E-W with N-S graves and even various intermediate variants. The reasons behind such variation are not always clear and in some cases it may simply be a way of picking out the burial of a more important individual and giving it special treatment. This can occur even in the seventh-century 'proto-Christian' cemeteries, as at Chamberlains Barn Cemetery II near Leighton Buzzard (Bedfordshire). Nevertheless, it is necessary to investigate whether there is a chronological or organizational pattern to those burials which share a particular orientation.

Further aspects of cemetery organization

We must also consider the distribution of the various body positions in which individuals have been buried, whether supine, crouched or prone, whether facing right or left, etc., to see whether a meaningful pattern emerges when plotted on to the cemetery plan and correlated with the age, sex and other data provided by the human biologist's report. Further information about gender can be obtained from the grave finds with certain types of dress-fittings being normally associated with women from the age of puberty onwards and weapons with men. From this we can establish whether the cemetery seems to have been organized into family burial plots, or whether men and women were buried in separate areas.

It should be noted that, while burials of babies and children of all ages do occur in both inhumation and cremation cemeteries, their numbers are relatively small compared to the size of the adult population. In other words, when infants and children died for whatever reason, they did not necessarily get accorded burial in the community cemetery. A majority of burials of both sexes seem to have died in their teens or early twenties, with the risks from childbirth and violent death in feuds and war to add to those of disease and accidents in this age group. But if you survived into your thirties, you seem to have had a good chance of reaching quite an advanced age and dying in your bed.

Cemetery sequences

A relative sequence pattern can be obtained from intercutting and superimposed graves, which provide a stratigraphical relationship, with one grave preceding the other. This is the case within Plot A at Buckland, Dover, which is subdivided into two phases of burial (nos.1 and 2). Another approach to sequencing is based on grouping together graves which share similar combinations of finds and plotting them on a plan to see if these groupings form coherent patterns. This method, rather misleadingly called horizontal stratigraphy, enables us to follow the development of a cemetery. Comparisons of the grave finds with those from other cemeteries, whose approximate date ranges have been established, further allow a particular stage of development to be attributed to a century or even to a fraction of a century.

In this way the Buckland cemetery finds have been divided by their excavator, Professor Vera Evison, into a series of phases (nos.1-3, each 50 years long, beginning in the late fifth to early sixth century, with nos.4-6 each 25 years long and no.7 attributed to the first half of the eighth century). Some object types were in use and were being deposited over more than one phase, but other types were restricted to a particular phase (52).

The Buckland sequence seems to represent a community of around ten individuals per generation buried within a small and constricted burial ground in phases 1 and 2 (53). This community suddenly expanded three-fold in phase 3 and its graves were dug away from, and mostly east of, the initial burial ground. A family burial plot on the northern edge of the cemetery in phases 3 to 5 was centred on a prehistoric barrow mound and ditch, as already mentioned (54). This barrow and the relative positions of a few isolated post-holes have been argued to have had an important role in laying out the cemetery (55), just as various post-holes at Yeavering were claimed to be used for aligning its buildings. Not everyone is as convinced as Buckland's excavator on this point, however.

Other information can be plotted on to the cemetery plan, such as correlations between the relative amount of labour and materials which have been expended on digging and constructing a grave, and the range of objects with which the individual buried was furnished. The presence of a ring-ditch cut into the subsoil around a grave, with its implication of a substantial mound over the burial, is straightforward enough, particularly if the grave is a large chamber affair as in one example at Spong Hill.

On the other hand, there are cases where a grave stands out as markedly isolated from its neighbours and we can suspect that a substantial earth mound formerly covered it, despite the absence of any ring-ditch demarcating it. Presumably the mound was respected by those subsequently digging graves in the same sector of the cemetery. When such a burial turns out to be exceptionally well furnished with objects, such a claim does not seem unreasonable.

52 *Object types which define the first two phases of the Buckland (Dover) cemetery: on the left weapons above keys and knives, in the middle brooches, beads and pendants above buckles, and on the right containers.*

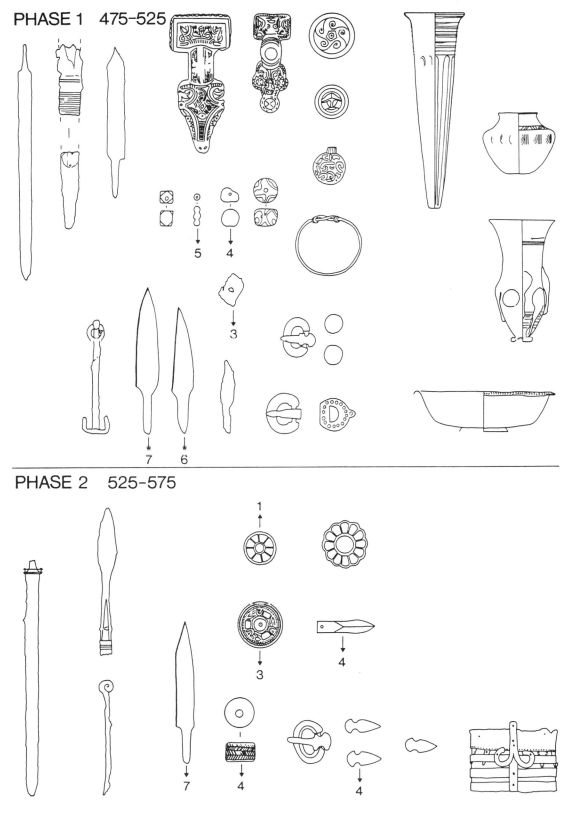

PHASE 1   475-525

PHASE 2   525-575

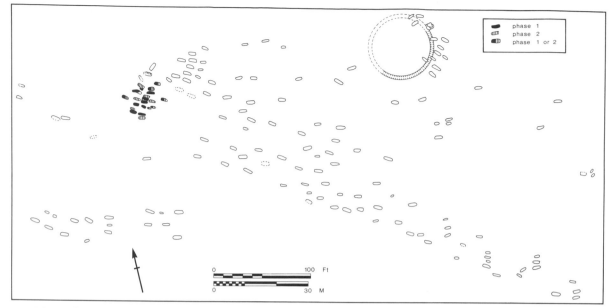

53 *Plan of the Buckland cemetery in phases 1 (AD 475–525) and 2 (AD 525–75).*

54 *Plan of the Buckland cemetery in phases 3 (AD 575–625), 4 (AD 625–50), 5 (AD 650–75), 6 (AD 675–700) and 7 (AD 700–50).*

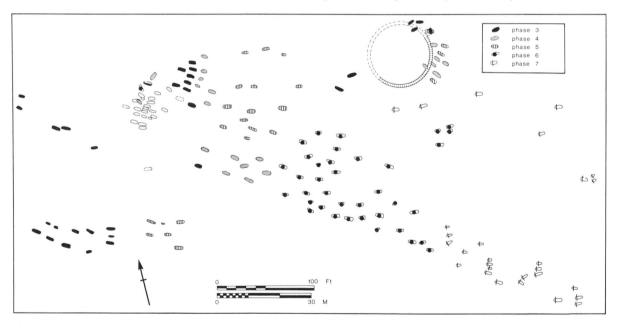

Barrows have been postulated on such grounds alone at Finglesham (see **51**) for instance a mound up to 12m (39ft) in diameter may have been constructed over the male burial of Grave 204. Careful re-examination of other cemetery plans may reveal many other examples in the future.

Where there is a substantial burial structure, but the grave itself has been robbed, we can suspect that it may have been relatively richly furnished. But we must not automatically expect to find a correlation between the grave size and construction and the finds. In a period, such as the later seventh and early eighth century, when grave finds appear to be going out of fashion under the influence of Christian

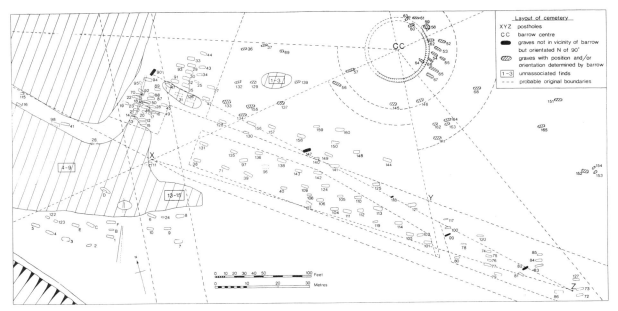

55 *Layout plan of the Buckland cemetery.*

ideology, elaborate grave structures may have provided an alternative and acceptable means of marking the status of individuals.

In considering correlations between grave depth and finds in ordinary 'coffin' burials, we should also be aware that the original land surface of the Anglo-Saxon period usually no longer exists, having been eroded away by subsequent plough-action. This makes it difficult to estimate how deeply the original grave cuts were dug. What we actually measure during an excavation is either the depth of the bottom of a grave below the top of the modern land surface, or more often the depth of the grave from the top of the subsoil into which it was dug. This reflects the fact that in an excavation it is not always possible to detect the outline of the grave cut in the churned-up topsoil. Only when the topsoil has been removed can we expect to see the grave fill against the background of undisturbed subsoil. Varying rates of plough damage may occur in different zones of a cemetery, particularly if part of it occupies sloping ground. Graves can be almost ploughed away in one area and yet remain relatively undamaged in another.

Grave finds
There are ready-made computer packages now available for analysing grave goods, one of which is based on the assumption that the richer burials will also contain many of the object types found in more ordinary 'poorer'

graves. A fairly large cemetery is required before it becomes worthwhile applying such computer techniques, or indeed most other statistical methods. A hundred graves is a working minimum, but two hundred or more is what is really needed.

Simpler approaches exist for smaller cemetery samples, such as creating by hand charts on graph paper. These order the finds by category, separating out the male from the female assemblages and starting with those with the largest numbers of objects, before working down to those accompanied by just a waist buckle or a knife. Thus with weapon graves, those with relatively rare and prestigious weapons, such as a long sword or an axe, would be listed ahead of those with a shield, which in turn would appear ahead of those accompanied by a spear only. The number and types of brooches and other dress-fittings would provide the basis for a similar chart of fifth- to sixth-century female assemblages (**56**).

Another approach is to list the number of object types which occur in each grave. With this system it does not matter how many brooches or beads were found with a burial, for a pair of brooches worn on the shoulders could be counted as just one object type, a single brooch on the chest as another object type and

a. Apple Down male inhumation assemblages, Cemetery 1

Grave no.	12A	63	99b	152	145	68	54	148B	163	31	67	113	122	121	123	126	12B	125	138A	22	46	55	62	25B	71	91	102	109
Sword	*																											
Seax		X																										
Shield			X	X	X																							
Spear		X	X	X	X	X	X	X	X	X	X	X	X	X	X	X	X	X										
Buckle		X	X	X		X	X	X		X	X	X	X						X	X	X	X	X					
Belt mounts																								X				
Purse					X																							
Firesteel		X			X			X																				
Tweezers	X																X											
Ring								X																				
Pin									X										X									
Single bead	X																X											
Knife		X	X	X	X	X	X	X	X	X	X	X	X	X	X				X	X	X	X	X		X	X	X	X
Bucket	*	X																										
Bowl/box						X																						

b. Apple Down female inhumation assemblages, Cemetery 1

Grave no.	14	10	13	128	48	86	151	88	33	165	170B	130	134	117	107	18	137B	23	78	97	93	11	50	108	157	72	44	87	169	175A
Large brooch	X																													
Brooch pair	X	X																												
Single small brooch			X	X	X																									
Pin/needle						X	X	X	X	X	X																			
Beads	X	X	X	X								X	X	X	X															
Single bead								X							X															
Coin		X												X		XX	X													
Finger ring		X	X				X	X					X																	
Buckle	X	X	X	X								X	X			X	X	X	X	X	X	X	X	X						
Belt mount																X														
Purse	X															X														
Tweezers																									X					
Toilet set					X																									
Comb																									X					
Knife	X	X	X			X	X	X	X	X	X	X					X	X	X						X	X	X	X		X
Antler tool			X																											
Mount														X																
Bowl/box																	X								X					
Potsherd																					X									

c. Apple Down, Cemetery 1

	Female children's inhumation assemblages					Unsexed children's inhumation assemblages							Unsexed adult's inhumation assemblages				
Grave no.	15	38	90	141	51	69	139	70	100	161	76	89	85	104	79	41A	164
Brooch	X																
Beads		X	X	X													
Single bead													X				
Coin													X				
Finger ring				X													
Bangle ring				X													
Buckle						X	X								XX	X	
Belt mount						X											
Knife								X	X	X	X			X		X	X
Bucket mount	X																
Pot											X	X					

56 *Charts of finds from graves in Apple Down Cemetery 1.*

a large string of beads as a third object type. As a means of simplifying and regularizing comparisons between different assemblages it seems to work well.

What has been much more controversial are

attempts to give scores or valuations to objects buried in graves, in order to compare the relative wealth of different cemeteries. Two researchers, John Shephard and Chris Arnold, have calculated a numerical value for each object type, giving a low score to commonplace items such as iron knives and a much higher score to glass vessels, and the highest value of all to helmets, which are extremely rare. The problem with this approach is that the range of objects worn on the clothing of the deceased or deposited in their graves was clearly carefully selected for that purpose and does not necessarily represent their true value among the belongings of an individual or family.

Also these researchers have not always been subtle enough, for Arnold valued all brooches as having the same score. Yet an examination of the total range, from brooches studded with garnets in gold or silver settings to plain copper alloy fittings, should indicate the need for a matching range of values. If this is not attempted, even comparisons between different contemporary cemeteries can become meaningless.

There is also the fact that the range of dress-fittings and other items deposited in graves changed over the centuries. Fifth-century burials are relatively poorly furnished with grave finds, whereas ostentation is typical of the sixth century, and this continues into the first half of the seventh century in Kent. Major changes occurred during the seventh century. Female dress saw brooches replaced by small linked pins used to fasten a head veil and there was a marked reduction in the burial of weapons and other items. Presumably these changes reflect the influence of contemporary fashion, seen in burials on the Continent with nominally Christian populations. We must take care to limit comparisons to contemporary cemeteries, so that like is compared with like.

An American scholar, Ellen-Jane Pader, has made a different contribution to the debate on the issue of the symbolic elements in burial rite. She has argued that the positioning of objects within the grave was not arbitrary, but made a social statement, which those burying the dead fully understood. Thus she believes that it is important to note whether a sword is placed on the right or the left side of the body and to see whether there are patterns in the layout of other graves containing swords within different sectors of a cemetery. Of course, sometimes these positions could simply reflect whether the deceased was right or left handed. In any case, it is not clear that we will ever understand how the Anglo-Saxons interpreted such symbolism. All we can do is to record the patterning as accurately as possible. In all probability its symbolic meaning will always elude us.

Social structure

The social interpretation of cemeteries remains to be tackled. Sonia Hawkes interprets the 25 sixth-century graves at Finglesham (a few more may have been destroyed by chalk pit workings) as representing an aristocratic family over two or three generations and their retainers and servants. The well-armed burial of Grave 204 is matched by the rich woman of Grave D3 buried c.525-30, while graves 203 and E2 belong to wealthy women buried sometime after 550. There seem to be no burials here appropriate to peasant farmers, whose labours would help to support such nobles. Perhaps sixth-century Finglesham is comparable to a small contemporary cemetery excavated in Switzerland at Basel-Bernerring. The aristocrats there were buried in large chamber graves across the centre of the burial ground, while their bodyguard and servants were placed in more modest 'coffin' burials to either side. There are no outstanding seventh-century rich graves among the remaining 218 burials at Finglesham, but rather more ordinary people were now inhumed here. Its nobles had moved on, as had the Basel community after three generations, or else rather less likely the family had become impoverished.

Interpreting the range of objects placed in different burials among these more ordinary farming communities presents a different type of problem. While it is tempting to group all the better furnished adult female and male burials as belonging to a single more successful family, it would seem that the hamlet settlements at Chalton and West Stow consisted of farm units of equal size and value. This would suggest that the better furnished graves represent the heads of each family in any given generation, who were given special treatment. If this is correct, then the quantity and quality of grave finds will reflect the relative status of individuals within their family farmstead.

In all probability, it was the head of the family who would organize the burial of their own folk and it would be the duty of their eldest son or daughter to do the honours when they died in turn. Items of family as well as personal property may well have been deposited in order to send off the more important members of the family. Recent analysis of a sixth-century cemetery of 117 burials at Norton-on-Tees has some 10 (but originally 12) weapon burials, matched by a similar number of well-dressed women over some three generations. This would give us eight well-furnished burials per generation for the heads of four family farmsteads, each with a household of nine or ten.

A similar interpretation has been offered by Jørgensen in analysing family burial clusters in cemeteries on the Danish island of Bornholm from the Roman period to the Viking Age. There the special treatment was restricted to just one partner of the married couple who were also heads of the family. If the woman died first, she may be buried with many brooches, but her spouse would not be accompanied by a full weapon set. But if he died first, the position would be reversed. No cases of this practice have yet been noted in England, where apparently both partners were buried with full honours as heads of the family.

Cremation cemeteries
Cremation cemeteries can also be analysed, though in less detail. Clusters of two or more pottery urns in a single pit imply a contemporary group, though many pots are placed in a single pit on their own. Then similarities in the decoration applied to pots enable excavators to link urns from different sectors of a burial ground. Stamp decoration is very fashionable on all ornamented pottery from the later fifth century and through the sixth century. The mechanical nature of stamped ornament permits us to be very precise in identifying a pot as the product of particular individual workshop. While some stamp designs are so commonplace (e.g. the cross-in-circle) that they are of little use in this respect, except when the stamp has been damaged in a unique way, other stamps can be extremely distinctive. Charts showing their combinations on various urns can be drawn up, as at Spong Hill, where some 67 groups of stamp-linked pots have already been identified (**60**).

On the whole, the stamped urns at Spong Hill were distributed around the edges of the cemetery, though a few were located nearer its centre (**59**). This is the pattern we might expect

from a cemetery founded in the fifth century and expanding out from that central core during the sixth century with its stamped pottery. Simple linear decoration and pushed-out bosses characterize the earlier decorated pottery here, and some examples are very similar to pots from urnfields in the continental homelands (**58**). Brooches and other small finds, both burnt and unburnt, which occur among the contents of more than half the urns help to confirm this pattern. Painstaking examination of distorted fragments of brooches, combs and glass vessels can identify diagnostic parts comparable to complete examples from inhumation grave contexts elsewhere. The earlier fifth-century brooch forms are found in the central area of the cemetery, while the later forms are out on the peripheries (**57**). Charts and distribution maps of different types of pottery decoration and object types from urns based on those from Spong Hill have now been published for several other urnfield cemeteries in eastern England.

The more elaborate stamps at Spong Hill include runic inscriptions bearing the name of a warrior god TIW and portrayals of animals, and it has been argued that these stamp combinations conveyed a message about the person being commemorated. This concept of heraldic-type devices, that perhaps told contemporaries the name of the deceased and his or her forbears, relies on us accepting that cremation pottery vessels were purpose-made for funerary use only. But what if they were simply the nicest-looking general storage pots available in any given household and were chosen because they were the favourite pots of the individuals concerned? Large, well-decorated pots occurred among the domestic pottery from the settlements at Mucking which were comparable to vessels used as urns in one of its cemeteries. For the time being, we have no way of knowing whether a particular urn was produced to

57, 58 & 59 *Plans of one segment of the Spong Hill (Norfolk) cemetery; the first shows the distribution of brooches from urns (the earliest being the cruciform group 1, 'stutzarm' and applied brooches); the second the location of pots with ornament similar to that on fifth-century urns in continental cemeteries; and the third stamp-linked pottery attributed to the sixth century. The earliest urns tend to be near the centre and later pots around the periphery of the cemetery.*

cruciform group I   "stutzarm"

cruciform group I/II   annular, penannular

other cruciform or small-long   applied

● vertical boss/groove

▲ rosette

■ arch/chevron, dot

◆ facet/slashing on carination

CEMETERY ANALYSIS AND SOCIAL STATUS

Stamp-linked pottery groups

●	1-3	▲	7
◗	4	◆	8
◖	5	■	12
⬣	6	⬢	9, 10, 13, 14

85

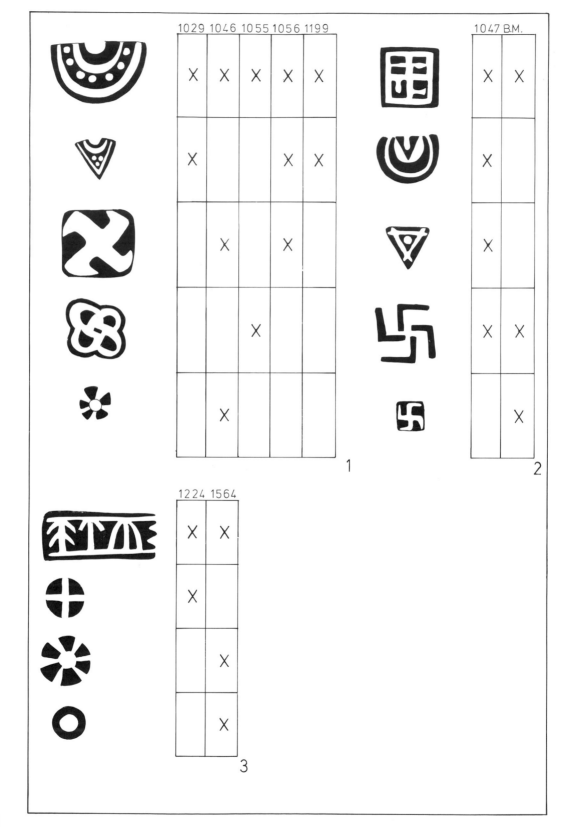

commission, while the person concerned lay on their death bed, or whether it came off the kitchen shelf.

With the large numbers of urns and the repetitive nature of their contents, statistical analysis using computers provides the obvious means of making sense of the data, thus enabling comparisons to be made between cemeteries. Julian Richards has carried out a pioneering study here, which has sought to establish correlations between sex and age groups, based on analysis of the cremated bone; the size, shape and decoration of the urns; the presence or absence of cremated animal bone; and the presence of various types of object among the contents. More research needs to be carried out and statistical approaches need to be developed further though it is interesting to see, for example, that the height of a pot seems to be related to the age of the deceased, but that adult males are usually deposited in taller vessels than adult females. This might be seen as an argument for urns being specially potted for burial purposes, but it need imply no more than a selection of suitable pots from the available storage vessels, in order to mark the sex and status. There also seem to be correlations between types of decoration on pots and the objects accompanying them. Both glass vessels and gaming pieces from board games seem to be associated with very tall pots and are seen as symbols of high status, as indeed they are when they occur in inhumation burials.

Serious study and analysis of cremation burials in England is still very much in its infancy and the full publication of the Spong Hill cemetery within the 1990s will provide an important landmark. It is not so clear whether we will be equally successful in creating techniques for analysis of mixed-rite cemeteries. Obviously we can observe where a cremation burial feature has been dug into or cuts through inhumation graves. We can also note where a pot or a brooch or some other object type occurs in both types of burial context. But in practice, we have to analyse all the cremations separately from the inhumations, as if they belonged to different cemeteries and then attempt to marry the results together.

At Spong Hill the sixth-century inhumation cemetery is distinctly separate, containing well-furnished graves and several burials within ring-ditches, including one chamber grave. It is certainly tempting to interpret this sector as belonging to a small aristocratic community of the Finglesham and Basel-Bern-erring type. Yet it would be dangerous to assume that the much larger cremation sector consisted of no more than the burials of peasant households. There is a late fifth-century cremation belonging to a woman, whose dress was fastened by a silver-gilt equal-arm brooch and a pair of cast saucer brooches, all probably manufactured in north-west Germany. These make her the social equal of any of the Spong Hill inhumation burials a generation or more later. Such ostentation is rare among cremation urn deposits, however, which makes detailed comparisons between inhumations and cremations difficult, perhaps impossible, even within a single cemetery.

60 *Chart illustrating pottery stamps of Spong Hill groups 1–3. These include a stamp with the three runic letters TIW – a god's name, while the swastika is a cult symbol linked particularly with Thunor.*

7

High-status burial and the emergence of kingdoms

Before we can identify individual Anglo-Saxon burials as belonging to kings or their nobility, we need to consider the size and power of the kingdoms emerging in the historical record from the later sixth and seventh centuries. Kings were primarily military leaders and their success depended on their ability to defeat or intimidate other rulers and extract tribute from them. Two or more kings might share the task of ruling a kingdom, though usually one of them was recognized as the senior partner. Sometimes the senior ruler is the father of the junior, but authority can be shared between brothers or cousins. Normally under such arrangements, each king was responsible for a separate region within the kingdom.

Anglo-Saxon kingdoms

The size of the kingdoms, or 'provinces' as Bede usually calls them, varied enormously. The largest kingdoms in the seventh century seem to have been the result of the amalgamation of many smaller provinces under a militarily successful royal family. There were four of these 'super kingdoms'. Each was ruled by at least one king who had succeeded in achieving overlordship as *brytenwealda* over most of the other Anglo-Saxon kingdoms during his reign.

For example, Northumbria was the result of an amalgamation of the two smaller kingdoms of Bernicia and Deira in north-east England. Under kings of the Bernician royal house this northern Anglian province expanded west and north to absorb the British kingdoms of Elmet and Rheged and much else besides during the seventh century. Similarly Penda and his descendants as kings of the Mercians expanded from an initial power base along the Middle Trent. Before the end of the seventh century

they came to rule the entire Midlands from Lindsey (Lincolnshire) to the Thames valley, including London, and from the Severn to the Cambridgeshire Fens. In the Fenlands and the East Midlands they competed with the powerful East Anglian kingdom, which added the Isle of Ely to its territory during that century.

The Mercians also drove the kings of the *Gewisse* out of their heartland in the Thames valley around Oxford. This forced Gewissan rulers to expand south and west, in the process creating a new West Saxon kingdom during the seventh century. Now based in Hampshire and Wiltshire, the West Saxon kings expanded west into Dorset, Somerset and Devon at the expense of the British and at the same time vied with the Mercians for control of Berkshire, Surrey and Sussex to the east.

These four major kingdoms survived into the ninth century and the Scandinavian invasions of the Viking period. By then they had absorbed all of the middle-ranking kingdoms of the seventh century. Kent was the largest of these and even as late as the eighth century its kings could dominate political events in south-east England. After the 610s though they found that they could no longer compete on equal terms with the big four. Many of these medium-sized kingdoms were approximately the size of modern counties, as with the South Saxons (West and East Sussex) and the East Saxons (Essex). The extent to which such kingdoms represent the simple takeover of a Romano-British *civitas* district, formerly administered from a town like Canterbury, remains uncertain. The Roman origin of the name for Kent is suggestive here, but its significance has perhaps been exaggerated.

There were also numerous smaller provinces

ruled by 'sub-kings' or 'princes' according to Bede and other sources. A substantial number of these were listed in a document called the *Tribal Hidage* and most of them can be located within the East Midlands and the Fenland islands, both from other written sources and place-name evidence. It is possible that the people in even the smallest provinces and regions normally addressed their rulers as kings. In their dealings with more powerful and dominant rulers of larger kingdoms such 'kings' were demoted to be sub-kings or princes. The earliest surviving copy of the *Tribal Hidage* was written in the eleventh century, but its list of Anglo-Saxon kingdoms and peoples (tribes) seems to refer to a seventh century situation. Perhaps it gives us a snapshot view of these smaller units just before they were swept up and absorbed into one of the greater kingdoms. But it is an incomplete list, for other written sources and place-names tell us of the existence of a significant number of similar political units, which fail to appear in the *Tribal Hidage*. An example is the *Hæstingas*, the people of the Hastings region (East Sussex). These tiny provinces are perhaps the building blocks from which many medium-sized and larger kingdoms were created by a mixture of military conquest and marriage alliances.

Peak District barrow burials

Some elements of this political picture can be seen in the archaeological record, though inevitably our evidence is patchy. In the case of the *Tribal Hidage*'s *Pecsætan*, we can equate the 'Peak dwellers' with a series of seventh-century barrow burials well furnished with grave finds within the limestone countryside of the White Peak in Derbyshire and Staffordshire. Unfortunately the majority of these were excavated or, often, looted in the eighteenth and nineteenth centuries.

One of them may well represent the burial of a 'prince', for the famous Benty Grange barrow contained among other things the remains of a helmet, an extremely rare find in Anglo-Saxon England. Its framework of iron bands was originally infilled with horn plates and it was ornamented with a silver and presumably Christian cross on the nose-guard. There is also a three-dimensional representation of a boar on the crest, which reminds us of the imagery of boars on helmets in the *Beowulf* poem. Another well-equipped man was buried under a barrow on Lapwing Hill accompanied by weapons and lying on a wooden bed, whose presence was revealed by its iron fittings. Rich female barrow graves accompanied by fine garnet-set gold dress-fittings also occurred, notably at Cow Low and White Low.

Evidence for bed burial as a special practice peculiar to the seventh century can be found in two other regions of England: around Cambridge and in Wiltshire. For example, recent excavations at the Barrington cemetery west of Cambridge have revealed two bed burials datable to the seventh century. As in the case of the Peak District graves, the West Saxon bed burials have been found exclusively with rich deposits under individual barrow mounds.

The Swallowcliffe Down barrow

The recently-published site on Swallowcliffe Down (Wiltshire) provides a good example. Unfortunately the grave of this young woman of 18-25 years had already been partially robbed of her finest dress-fittings, probably in the nineteenth century (**61**). Nevertheless meticulous recording by the excavators during the 1966 investigation permitted accurate reconstruction of many features of her burial (**62**). She was accompanied by an iron-bound yew-wood bucket and an iron pan at the head end, while at the foot of the grave there was a bronze-mounted bucket. By her left thigh there was a maple-wood casket with bronze fittings and its miscellaneous contents, together with a leather satchel on the right side of the body and two glass cups by her right forearm.

The rich dress assemblage recovered from another Wiltshire barrow on Roundway Down shows the sort of fittings which might well have been removed by nineteenth-century barrow diggers from the Swallowcliffe burial. A pair of delicate gold pins with a single garnet set in the head of each are linked by gold chains to a central glass setting of probable Irish manufacture. This is accompanied by a series of gold metal beads and garnet cabochon gold pendants which formed a collar typical of wealthy female dress in the second half of the seventh century (**colour plate 4**).

Male counterparts to these rich women are represented among contemporary excavated barrow burials, for example at Ford, Laverstock near Salisbury and Lowbury Hill in Berkshire. Both were accompanied by shields with a tall iron cone-shaped boss to protect the handgrip,

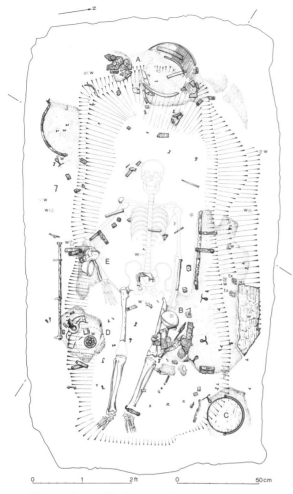

61 *Plan of a robbed seventh-century barrow burial of a noble woman on Swallowcliffe Down (Wilts.)*

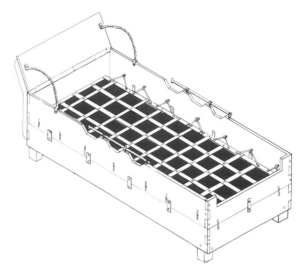

62 *Reconstruction of the wooden bed from the Swallowcliffe Down grave.*

63 *A bronze hanging-bowl which contained crab apples and onions recovered from a seventh-century weapon grave under a barrow at Ford, Laverstock (Wilts.).*

which is a form typical of this period (the so-called sugar-loaf boss) and bronze vessels called hanging-bowls (63). At Ford these were associated with a short single-bladed sword called a seax, buried in its silver-fitted leather scabbard, a Frankish weapon-type which became fashionable in England during the seventh century. There was also a pair of spears. The Lowbury Hill man had a long sword and a single spear as his weapons. Presumably such burials represent the graves of local noblemen and women, placed prominently in the landscape, as befitted their role as landowners and kept separate from the cemeteries in which the farming communities were buried.

In Kent, as in the Cambridge region, the equivalent burials tend to be found in communal cemeteries, rather than as isolated barrow burials. There are exceptions though, as with the seventh-century barrow burial containing a fine pair of decorated casket mounts from Allington Hill near Cambridge. Similarly at Coombe in north-east Kent, a late sixth-century weapon assemblage was associated with an apparently isolated cremation deposit in a bronze bowl excavated around 1845. It is not known whether the Coombe finds were buried beneath a barrow or not. Certainly the presence of a sixth-century brooch and beads suggest a double burial of a man and a woman, or even imply that part of a separate female burial had also been disturbed by the excavators. The

90

finely ornamented sword was apparently accompanied by a second sword, a spear and possibly even an axe, implying the burial of a noble man, perhaps even a 'prince'.

Sutton Hoo Mound 1

Much grander weapon assemblages are represented by the burials from Taplow overlooking the Thames (Buckinghamshire) excavated in 1882; Broomfield near Chelmsford (Essex) discovered in 1888 and further excavated in 1894; and the great Sutton Hoo ship burial in mound 1 opposite Woodbridge (Suffolk), first investigated in 1939. Finds from all three sites are to be found side by side on display in the British Museum. Royal status has been attributed to the Sutton Hoo deposit and it has been claimed as the grave of Rædwald king of the East Anglians. His death occurred some time after his victory over Æthelfrith king of the Northumbrians in 616 or 617 as recorded by Bede. A much later written source places his death, not implausibly, in 624 or 625.

Certainly Sutton Hoo mound 1 contained the burial of a rich and powerful man (**colour plate 5**). The earliest date at which the last Frankish gold coin to be minted might have got into his purse has been calculated as somewhere between 622 and 629. It remains by far the grandest and most wealthy grave assemblage of the Anglo-Saxon period yet excavated. On the other hand, it contains no inscription or signet ring to identify by name or title the person commemorated there and some caution is necessary before assigning it to a king of the East Anglians, let alone attributing it specifically to Rædwald.

By contrast, the grave of a fifth-century king of the Franks called Childeric has been successfully identified. This was accidentally discovered and looted in 1653 at Tournai (Belgium) and contained a signet ring bearing his name and rank in Latin as CHILDERICI REGIS. This symbol of authority would have been used to seal and authenticate his written orders and letters (**64**). According to the *History* of Gregory of Tours written a century later, the accession of his son Clovis took place in 481 or 482. Fortunately the collection of a hundred or so gold coins issued by emperors of the Eastern Roman Empire in Childeric's purse seem to justify a date around then. It is this level of confirmation that we lack for the identity of the man buried in Sutton Hoo mound 1, or

64 *A replica of the now-lost gold signet finger ring attributed to Childeric, king of the Franks who died in 481 or 482 and an impression taken from it.*

indeed for other members of what we presume to be the same family buried in a barrow cemetery of 20 or more mounds.

Much has been made of the so-called 'regalia' from the Sutton Hoo ship burial, but the case for treating them as royal insignia, let alone as symbols of the power and authority of an overlord king or *brytenwealda* is a tenuous one. Bede tells us that the Northumbrian Edwin had a *tufa* carried before him in the Roman manner as he progressed around his kingdom. However, Bede failed to describe the physical appearance of this 'standard'. We certainly have no right to assume that the iron stand from Sutton Hoo represents a similar *tufa* belonging to the Rædwald, who defeated Æthelfrith and made Edwin king of the Northumbrians. Indeed the Sutton Hoo stand may be no more than an elaborate portable lampstand. Surely any imitation of a Roman army standard would have been decorated in precious metals.

Then, while no one can doubt that the ornamental whetstone is a symbolic object which had never been used to sharpen an iron blade, this does not make it a royal sceptre. Indeed, if the bronze ring and stag should turn out *not* to have been attached at one end, we have an object which is rather less sceptre-like. The eight bearded and beardless heads portrayed on it might be gods, heroes or the ancestors of the deceased. Perhaps this whetstone should be seen as a private family totem rather than as a public symbol of office.

German archaeologists have a useful term for burials of the Sutton Hoo, Taplow and Broomfield type. They are described as princely graves (*Fürstengräber*), which implies a certain level of power and wealth but is not too explicit as to the precise authority and family identity of the individual. The rank above is that of royal graves (*Königsgräber*), which ideally require the level of identification provided by the Tournai Childeric burial, while the next rank below princely graves is that of noble graves (*Adelsgräber*).

Sutton Hoo and Taplow

Certainly the furnishings of these 'princely' burials at Sutton Hoo and Taplow illustrate a lifestyle which fits royal and aristocratic society as portrayed in heroic poetry, above all in *Beowulf*. These are men accompanied by sets of weapons and armour as befit important warriors who could command warbands or even small armies. The Sutton Hoo burial contained an elaborate helmet of Scandinavian type, which in turn was based on a fourth-century Roman cavalry parade helmet form. There was also a large shield with intricate gold and gilded decorative ornaments, again of Scandinavian type, a tunic probably of leather with fine gold and garnet shoulder clasps which echo Roman parade armour, as well as a coat of mail. The corpse was also accompanied by a finely-decorated sword, a battle axe with an iron handle and an impressive collection of spears to be used both as thrown missiles and as thrusting weapons.

The sword may have originally been forged in the Frankish Rhineland and its garnet-decorated pommel may also be Frankish work. It is also possible that the fine gold sword- and belt-fittings set with garnets and glass, attributed to a 'Sutton Hoo master' craftsman, were the products of a Frankish-trained goldsmith. The large hollow gold buckle has a Frankish form and might have been made on the Continent to hold a Christian relic. All the gold coins in the purse are Frankish and the Mediterranean silverware and bronze 'Coptic' bowl presumably passed through Frankish territories before reaching Suffolk. But although the Frankish contribution to the Sutton Hoo ship burial should not be underestimated, it must be significant that the helmet does not belong to a continental type, as found in Frankish and Alamannic aristocratic and princely graves of the late sixth and early seventh centuries, such as Morken and Niederstotzingen (Germany).

Although the Taplow man lacked the helmet or armour of Sutton Hoo, he too was accompanied by a sword, three shields and several spears including a throwing javelin. Perhaps the three shields might be linked to later Scandinavian laws, which permitted the use of up to three shields during a formal legal duel. Alternatively the multiplicity of spears and shields could be thought of as equipment supplied for the use of a bodyguard. In either case, a significant statement about the social standing of this individual is being made.

The 27m (89ft) long wooden ship in which the Sutton Hoo warlord was buried was another measure of his power and influence. A wooden roofed chamber similar to one carved on a gravestone on the Baltic island of Gotland had been assembled across the middle of this large sea-going rowing boat to house the burial assemblage. Its construction destroyed the evidence from the gunwale of the boat which might have told us how many oarsmen were required to power this warship. The 37 gold coins and three blank gold discs from the purse collection may well represent a symbolic payment to an imaginary crew of 40 men who would row their lord to the world of the gods. This ingenious suggestion still provides the most convincing explanation yet offered for the selection of gold items in the purse collection with the two gold ingots being payment for the ship's master, the steersman.

Sutton Hoo Mound 2

A second barrow mound at Sutton Hoo also incorporated a clinker-built boat revealed by the characteristic iron rivets used to fasten one overlapping oak plank to the next. Recent re-excavation of this mound (**65**), previously investigated in 1938, however, revealed that the burial itself was placed in a separate rectangular wooden chamber. This had been broken into and badly disturbed by earlier excavators, perhaps in the nineteenth century. Chemical traces in the soil indicate the possible position of the unburnt body as crouched at the west end of the chamber. The boat or ship had been deposited above this chamber and its rivets dispersed either side of the mound by the nineteenth-century looters.

Various objects or fragments, which the grave robbers had left behind, reveal that a rich male burial had been deposited in the chamber. They included part of a sword blade and a blue glass vase. A precise match exists between decorated metal mounts for a drinking horn there and the pair in the mound 1 ship

65 *View of the base of the wooden grave chamber at Sutton Hoo Mound 2 (Suffolk) as excavated in 1989. (Sutton Hoo Research Trust.)*

burial. There are also similarities between the iron tubs from both burial chambers. In other words, the two men buried with boats under barrows are archaeologically contemporary. They contrast with the burial practice represented at the centre of four or more other mounds at Sutton Hoo (nos. 4, 5, 6 and 18), in which cremations were deposited in bronze bowls, as in the cremation deposit discovered at Coombe (Kent).

The Snape ship burial
The Sutton Hoo barrows may have dominated the skyline to any boat passing up or down the river Deben, reminding them of the power of the family whose ancestors were buried there. Similarly the five or more barrows sited some 18km (11 miles) to the north-east near Snape

overlooked the river Alde. One of these contained a clinker-built boat, 15m (48ft) long, excavated in 1862 or 1863, whose contents seem to have been already disturbed. They included a glass claw-beaker and a fine gold finger-ring, both possibly imported from the Frankish Rhineland and implying burial around the middle, and no later than the second half, of the sixth century.

Recent excavation has revealed two much smaller boat-graves within the Snape cemetery which included these barrows. They contained dug-out canoes of a type found in the second-to third-century graves of the Slusegard cemetery on the Baltic island of Bornholm. Admittedly these boat-graves do not seem to have been marked by a mound, but they do re-emphasize the archaeological links between the east coast of Suffolk and the islands off the coast of Sweden already noted from Sutton Hoo. Boat burial seems to have been brought to England by Scandinavian settlers and seems so far to be restricted to East Anglia. It should be noted though that, while it contained no boat, the isolated Taplow barrow mound would have dominated its section of the river Thames in much the same manner as the Suffolk barrows would have done.

Royal society
Kings and princes were expected to reward their followers with gifts of weapons, armour and gold according to *Beowulf*. Their hospitality included feasting, and both the Sutton Hoo and Taplow burials contain pairs of ornamented drinking horns and a wide variety of vessels for the preparation, storage and serving of alcoholic drinks and food. The presence of stringed musical instruments called lyres to accompany the recitation of poetry and song, as well as gaming pieces for board games provide a commentary on the life of the warrior in peacetime. The motif of a bird of prey alighting on a duck from the Sutton Hoo purse may reflect another aspect of a princely and aristocratic lifestyle by portraying the art of falconry. The thrusting spears in these graves could also be used in hunting. Admittedly lacking from these burials is the bone evidence for hunting dogs, hawks and horses found in the mainland Swedish boat mounds at Vendel and Valsgärde, together with helmets and shields which are poor relations of those in the Sutton Hoo ship burial. Nevertheless we can

imagine it as an important activity in Anglo-Saxon aristocratic households.

Who was buried at Sutton Hoo?

Also lacking are the physical remains of the corpse in the Sutton Hoo ship burial, which in all probability were removed by the acidic effects of the sandy soil at this site. Unfortunately the type of chemical soil tests which recently revealed a possible impression of a body in the mound 2 chamber were simply not available in 1939. Textiles preserved in metal corrosion products suggest that the body would have been laid out on and covered with blankets and pillows, reminding us of the phenomenon of bed burial. The iron cleats found either side of the 'body space' seem to have been used to fasten together a high platform of planking on which the corpse lay.

While we cannot entirely rule out an ingenious suggestion that the Sutton Hoo warrior had been cremated and his 'ashes' placed on a large silver dish there, the close comparison between the layout of the Sutton Hoo and Taplow assemblages does make inhumation seem much more probable. Enough of the Taplow skeleton survived to demonstrate the mode of burial there. Although there are some discrepancies between the different plans made at the time of the Taplow excavation, or shortly after, the general placement of objects around the body share a lot in common with the dispositions around the 'body space' within Sutton Hoo mound 1 (**66**).

Broomfield

Similarly the Broomfield chamber grave aligned on an ESE-WNW axis contained a finely-decorated sword and buckle together with a spear and knife in its northern half, disturbed by workmen in 1888. The subsequent archaeological excavation in 1894 of the southern part of the grave produced the remains of a shield and an imported pottery vessel from an area adjacent to the findspots of the weapon set. Elsewhere there was a bronze vessel resting on a some folded textiles, which contained the tips of two cow's horns, two blue glass vases, which resemble the one recovered from Sutton Hoo mound 2 in 1938, and two wooden cups with metal rims and nearby two iron-bound wooden buckets, a small iron lampstand which resembles one from the Sutton Hoo ship burial and a large iron cauldron.

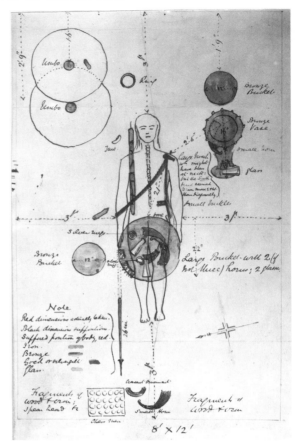

66 *Plan of the 'princely' chamber grave incompetently excavated in 1882 under a barrow mound in Taplow churchyard (Bucks.). This important discovery contained the most complete 'princely grave' assemblage until the famous Sutton Hoo burial.*

Human sacrifice?

One peculiar feature has been noted associated with a group of unfurnished inhumation graves inserted in and around cremation mound 5 at Sutton Hoo. Four of them were dug into open quarry pits at the edge of the mound, one of which already contained a deposit of animal bone. As seven of these 12 burials have been claimed to reveal evidence of ritual killing, it may be that human sacrifice was being practised in association with the burial rite of the family for whom the mounds were constructed.

Something similar has been claimed in the case of a discovery made in 1847 at Cuddesdon in Oxfordshire. A deposit of the type associated elsewhere with 'princely' burials and which

67 *Blue glass vase, one of two recovered from the Cuddesdon (Oxon.) 'princely' grave in 1847.*

contained among other things a bronze pail, two blue glass vases of the type found at Broomfield and Sutton Hoo mound 2 (**67**) and two swords, was located 'near' a small number of burials. These inhumations had been placed face down and arranged in a circle with their heads facing outwards and their legs crossed. They might conceivably represent human sacrifices associated with an early seventh-century 'princely' grave there, but the published account of their discovery is so ambiguous that little more can be said.

Rendlesham and Sutton Hoo

One aspect of the Sutton Hoo site that has particularly encouraged the speculation over whether it is the burial ground of the *Wuffingas* dynasty, which ruled the East Anglians in the later sixth and seventh centuries, is its supposed proximity to Rendlesham, which Bede informs us was the site of a royal *villa*. Yet the modern settlement centre of Rendlesham parish is some 6km (4 miles) away and there are good archaeological grounds for believing that the big house immediately north of the Sutton Hoo burial ground marks the site of a contemporary Anglo-Saxon settlement. Unless this is accepted as the site of the Rendlesham villa, there is no particular reason to link the Sutton Hoo burial ground to Bede's brief reference. As it is not

known how many royal *villae* and *vici* there were in seventh-century East Anglia, we should certainly be careful not to exaggerate the importance of the only one which Bede happens to mention in passing.

Of course, it is possible that the 'official' interpretation is correct and mound 1 was the burial place of the last pagan East Anglian king. Yet it is perhaps more by intuition than judgement that this conclusion has been reached. In fact we cannot state on the present evidence which region within East Anglia actually provided the power-base for the *Wuffingas* family; it does not need to have been in the Sandlings of south-east Suffolk.

An alternative view might suggest that each of the major river valleys around the Suffolk coastline could once have possessed a cemetery which contained rich barrow burials. Some will have been laid in or under a boat, emphasizing the Scandinavian origins and contacts of many settlers. In the sixth century we would expect these barrows to be grouped within a communal cemetery, as at Snape overlooking the Alde. We can compare their layout to the location of sixth-century barrow burials on one edge of the Spong Hill cremation cemetery in Norfolk. From the late sixth and early seventh century onwards both 'princely' and 'noble' barrows were normally separated from communal cemeteries, in family burial grounds as at Sutton Hoo, or in isolated mounds as at Taplow, Benty Grange and Swallowcliffe Down.

Did each of these Suffolk burial grounds belong to a separate powerful family, whose influence was primarily limited to the valley territory it dominated? A barrow excavated on Bloodmoor Hill near Lowestoft in 1758, containing finds which imply a rich seventh-century female burial, provides possible corroboration for this suggestion. It must have overlooked the coast as well as the river Waveney and Oulton Broad. If another barrow cemetery is ever discovered in the valleys of the Stour, the Gipping or the Blyth, we will certainly need to take this possibility seriously. Alternatively, perhaps the Snape barrows contained the sixth-century ancestors of those deposited in the mounds of the Sutton Hoo 'princely' cemetery in the first half of the seventh century.

It would seem that rich burials of 'princely' type were a physical manifestation of increased competition between the élites of kingdoms and provinces, which were being amalgamated into ever-larger political units and military alliances from the mid-sixth century onwards. Together with the establishment of élite rural settlements of the Yeavering type from the late sixth century onwards, they represent the emergence of a marked stratification of society, in which the most powerful differentiated themselves from the rest of society in death as in life.

Of course, only a relatively small number of élite burials have been recovered or recorded by modern archaeologists and earlier antiquarians. It would be rash to assume that the Coombe male cremation assemblage necessarily represents a member of the *Oiscingas* dynasty of Kent, that the Broomfield inhumation was a king or prince of the East Saxon royal house, or that the cremation deposit under the barrow at Asthall (Oxfordshire) on the edge of the Wychwood Forest commemorated a seventh-century prince (or princess) of the *Hwicce*.

Who was buried at Taplow?

From Æthelberht onwards, all Kentish kings seem normally to have been buried in mortuary chapels attached to Christian churches, though none of these has survived to be investigated scientifically. Equally, no certain burial of their pagan ancestors is known, though in a forthcoming publication a strong case will be made that the Taplow barrow represents the burial of a Kentish 'prince', who controlled the Thames valley west of London on behalf of the king of Kent. Leslie Webster is not the first scholar to note the Kentish nature of the buckle, clasps and other fittings at Taplow. She does go a step further, though, by observing that the Kentish objects belong to two different generations of production. Indeed there seems to be nothing present which would be out of place in a Kentish burial of that date. If the occupant had been a local ruler, who had accepted Kentish overlordship and received Kentish gifts, we might have expected to find some local non-Kentish objects as well.

As Leslie Webster also points out, the record of a land grant made between 672 and 674, provides an important clue as to the sort of authority and title that the Taplow 'prince' might have exercised. Frithuwold ruled the province of the men of Surrey as a sub-king of Wulfhere, king of the Mercians. This Frithuwold may have been the only recorded member of a local Surrey dynasty, reduced to the rank of a 'sub-king' by the Mercian overlord. It seems more probable though that he belonged to a successful noble family, whose members shared names beginning in Frith- and who controlled large territories from the East Midlands south to the Thames valley.

Frithuwold would seem to be a trusted 'sub-king' from the Midlands, appointed by Wulfhere to rule Surrey on his behalf, together with some other adjacent provinces. By this period, noble governors of provinces such as Frithuwold would be buried in mortuary chapels, just like their royal masters. The authority of their pagan antecedents would be better marked by barrow burial, dominating a major routeway, often a river as at Taplow. Sadly we can no longer refer to the Taplow Kentish 'prince' by name as Tæppa.

Claims for such an identification have been based on a belief that the place-name of Taplow refers to the *hlœw* or 'low' (mound) of Tæppa. Yet the first record of the place-name does not occur until the Domesday Book of 1086. So the barrow may have gained this title much later than the date of the burial it contained. Indeed Tæppa might well have been the name of a Late Saxon owner of the estate, which subsequently became the parish of Taplow. Similarly the Swallowcliffe Down barrow is referred to as *Posses hlœwe* in a charter of 940. Any personal name derived from it would have to be masculine, yet the occupant of the barrow grave was a young woman. Once again it seems more probable that the name refers to a pre-940 male landowner and that this barrow functioned as a boundary marker to his estate.

How many other recorded isolated 'princely' burials similarly commemorate the transitory rule of governors installed by overlords from other kingdoms? Clearly it is a possibility we can no longer afford to ignore.

1 Reconstruction of the Yeavering (Northumberland) royal villa during Edwin's visit. In the foreground cattle are corralled in the Great Enclosure, and a hunting expedition is assembling between the main hall and tents, in which members of the royal household who could not be accommodated in permanent timber buildings can sleep. In the background Paulinus leads local people from a grandstand, where they have heard Christ's message, down to the river Glen to receive a cold baptism. (Peter Dunn.)

2-3 Clusters of cremation urns from Spong Hill (Norfolk) in pits with stone settings. (Landscape Archaeology Section, Norfolk Museums Service.)

4 Gold pin set, with garnets in the pinheads and an inlaid glass stud at the centre of the linking chain. Recovered from the barrow burial of a rich seventh-century woman together with gold and garnet and gold beads on Roundway Down. (Wiltshire Archaeological & Natural History Society, Devizes.)

5 Reconstruction of the final stages of furnishing the princely or royal burial in the wooden chamber of the Sutton Hoo (Suffolk) mound 1 ship in the 620s or 630s. A leather jerkin with a fine pair of gold shoulder clasps attached seems to have been suspended from the chamber roof. (Peter Dunn.)

6 Reconstruction of Canterbury (Kent) in the fifth century, with small clusters of Anglo-Saxon *Grubenhäuser* among the ruins of abandoned Roman buildings. (© Canterbury Heritage Museum.)

7 Reconstruction of *Hamwic* in the eighth and ninth centuries. Trading ships would be drawn up along the beach of the Itchen near its confluence with the Solent. The boundary ditch at the settlement edge and the layout of gravelled streets and property plots containing houses, workshops, walls and rubbish pits, are all based on excavated evidence. (Southampton City Council.)

8 Reconstruction of the seventh- to ninth-century monastery at Jarrow (Tyne and Wear), Bede's home, based on the surviving church and the buildings excavated there. (Peter Dunn. © The Bede Monastery Museum, Jarrow.)

9 Reconstruction of the tenth-century residence of a thegn or noble, which occupied one corner of the Late Roman Saxon Shore fort of Portchester Castle (Hampshire). A bell may have been mounted on the stone tower which possibly was a church. (Peter Dunn.)

8

From Roman Britain to Anglo-Saxon England

Once, the creation of England would have been seen simply as a result of fifth-century conquest and mass migration by Anglo-Saxons flooding across the North Sea in clinker-built warships. The British in the eastern regions were driven out of their homes, fleeing west towards the south-west, Wales, Lancashire and Cumbria. In turn, they sparked off a migration from western Britain to Armorica, creating Brittany in north-west France.

Meanwhile, according to this view, the Anglo-Saxons created small kingdoms in the east and south, colonizing and farming a largely deserted landscape, founding new settlements with English place-names. The British who remained were enslaved. Military expansion of the first Anglo-Saxon kingdoms during the later sixth and seventh centuries was achieved mainly at the expense of British kingdoms to the west and north. The establishment of a fixed frontier with the Welsh kingdoms in the eighth century (Offa's Dyke; see **87**) and the conquest of Cornwall by Wessex in the ninth century mark the end of this sequence.

The Saxon Shore
An alternative view developed in reaction. This saw the process in terms of overlap and continuity, rather than disruption and discontinuity. As the Late Roman army recruited large numbers of barbarians from beyond its frontiers, it has been argued that significant numbers of troops recruited from north Germany were stationed in eastern and southern Britain during the fourth and early fifth centuries, if not earlier. Emphasis was now placed on apparent concentrations of Anglo-Saxon cemeteries around Roman towns. It was suggested that the Saxon Shore (*Litus Saxonicum*), a

defensive chain of Late Roman coastal forts between the Wash and Portsmouth Harbour, was so named because Saxon troops were employed to defend it (**68**). All this was argued principally from archaeological evidence, which it was claimed could be used to rewrite the history of the Anglo-Saxon settlements.

Caistor-by-Norwich
Similarities were seen between a rather small number of cremation urns found in just a few Anglo-Saxon cemeteries in eastern England and pots dated to the late third or fourth centuries from urnfields in north Germany and south Scandinavia. For example, a number of urns from the Caistor-by-Norwich cemetery were claimed to closely resemble pottery from urnfields on the Danish Baltic island of Fyn (or Fünen). As many of the urns from Fyn had handles and the Caistor pots lacked handles, the degree of similarity may have been exaggerated. Certainly before such early dates for the Caistor urns are accepted, we need to be aware of the Danish and German archaeologists' schemes for dating pottery. Basically, they remain reliant on finding pots in graves or hoards which also contained datable imported goods from the Roman Empire. Alternatively pots might be accompanied by other native objects, such as brooches, which have been dated from Roman imports when found together in other hoards or graves.

The Roman objects are datable because they are found within the Roman Empire together with Roman coins or inscriptions. These name particular emperors or officials and sometimes also carry a maker's stamp. In fact, the chain of associations linking cremation urns on Fyn to datable Roman goods does not allow for too

68 *The Saxon Shore fort of Burgh Castle (Suffolk). The curved ditch in the lower right-hand corner belongs to a later Norman castle. (Cambridge University Collection: copyright reserved)*

much precision about the probable date range within which the native pots were made and buried. Roman imports might have been kept as treasured items for some time before they were buried in Scandinavia. Finally, although there were changes in pottery shapes and decoration over the centuries in north Germany and south Scandinavia, the pace of change was often slow. The latest date for a particular type of pottery vessel is just as significant as the earliest possible date.

Of course, if just one south Scandinavian brooch or object datable to the fourth century had been found among the contents of the 'early' Caistor urns, there would be no reason to question their date (**69**). Yet not one single

Anglo-Saxon pottery urn from England can be shown to be earlier than the fifth century from the brooches or other finds they contained. On the other hand, at least one pot similar to one of the early Caistor urns has been found in a north German cemetery together with a fifth-century German brooch.

Nor is it likely that the Caistor cemetery co-existed for a century or more with the adjacent Roman town. If it had, we would expect to find everyday Late Roman objects in the cemetery. There are indeed a few Roman pots there, which the Anglo-Saxons have put to use as cremation containers. Yet these had been manufactured in the second century at the latest and almost certainly had been scavenged from a long abandoned Roman pottery kiln. Such reuse of old Roman material could take place as easily in the sixth or seventh centuries as in the fourth of fifth centuries.

The Roman town should also contain characteristic Anglian objects of the fourth century,

69 *Urn P15 from the Caistor-by-Norwich Anglo-Saxon cemetery. The late third- to fourth-century date attributed in the published report is much too early and it is unlikely to predate the fifth century.*

but none have been found as yet, though there is excavated evidence for Roman occupation there throughout the fourth century. So it seems that industrially-produced Roman pottery was no longer available when Anglo-Saxons came to settle next to this Roman town. By then, it seems probable that Caistor had been effectively abandoned, with no further organized urban life. In other words, there seems to have been a significant time-lapse between the abandonment of the Roman town and the first burials in the adjacent Anglo-Saxon cemetery, which seem to belong no earlier than the fifth century.

'Romano-Saxon' pottery

Another piece of evidence that has been used to justify extensive Anglo-Saxon settlement in eastern Britain during the fourth century has turned out to be even more unreliable. A type of Romano-British wheelthrown pottery seemed to be decorated in a similar manner to some handmade Anglo-Saxon cremation urns. The ornamentation concerned included bosses and also linear and rosette designs. It was suggested in the 1940s that they were made by British potters specifically for Anglo-Saxons, who requested pottery similar to their own with the same 'barbaric' ornamental schemes. On this basis, the pottery was labelled 'Romano-Saxon' (**70**) and regarded as positive evidence for Saxon settlement along and behind the

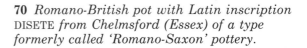

70 *Romano-British pot with Latin inscription* DISETE *from Chelmsford (Essex) of a type formerly called 'Romano-Saxon' pottery.*

shelter of the Late Roman Saxon Shore defences.

Recent research has shown that any influence went the other way round, from the Romans to the Saxons. Some of the kilns which produced 'Romano-Saxon' pottery have been excavated now in Hertfordshire and its production can be firmly dated to the third and fourth centuries. The range of decorative devices used on it belongs entirely within the mainstream Roman pottery repertoire. Many of them represent ceramic versions of ornamented silver vessels and mould-blown glassware. At the same time, the Anglo-Saxon pots they are supposed to be imitating had not yet been conceived, for none of the handmade versions in north Germany can be dated any earlier than the fifth century. It seems likely that Roman silverware and glass vessels also provided the models for the Anglo-Saxon potters.

There is nothing else to link the so-called 'Romano-Saxon' pottery to the Anglo-Saxons. No complete pots of this type have ever been found to accompany an Anglo-Saxon burial or building. There were a few small fragments of this pottery in a couple of *Grubenhäuser* at

71 *Reconstruction of a fifth-century Roman officer's broad belt with bronze buckle and other fittings from a grave by the Dyke Hills earthwork at Dorchester (Oxon.). Perhaps the burial of a Saxon mercenary commander with previous Roman military experience, who had been billeted here by a British 'tyrant'.*

Mucking (Essex), but these may well have been dumped in a Roman field with manure perhaps a century or more earlier and then accidentally transferred into the Anglo-Saxon pits, back-filled with local ploughsoil.

It seems then that the case for regarding the Saxon Shore as a coastal region of Britain settled in the fourth century by Saxons under Roman control has been built on quicksand. We should note that the Late Roman river defences along the Danube were called the Gothic bank (*Ripa Gothica*), because they were fortified against the Goths. Presumably the Saxon Shore was similarly constructed to limit and control sea raiding by Saxons.

Barbarians in the Roman army

Of course, there is every reason to believe that Franks, Alamans, Goths and other barbarian peoples recruited into the Roman army saw service in the provinces of Britain as late as the first decade of the fifth century. Their graves can be identified in Roman cemeteries in Britain, and it seems that these foreign soldiers also brought their wives and families with them. Examples occur at Winchester, to the north of the Roman town of *Venta Belgarum* on the site of Lankhills School. There were a number of graves containing men buried wearing crossbow brooches as cloak fasteners on the shoulder and metal fittings for a leather belt, which appear to be a part of their uniform. These brooches and belt sets seem to have been manufactured in imperial factories for official use.

We know that to receive or return a bronze-mounted broad leather belt (*cingulum*) was to accept or resign office in imperial service (**71**). Such belts were worn by both army officers and civil servants, but then they all held military ranks. When found in graves together with sets of weapons, such as spears, axes, swords and shield fittings, there is good reason to think that they belonged to army officers. In the case of the Lankhills burials they were accompanied by knives, so we cannot be certain that these men were soldiers, but it does seem probable. Roman officers are shown wearing such fittings on sculptures and wall paintings, but it seems that it was not Roman custom to be buried wearing these symbols of office. That was probably something that differentiated them from barbarian officers of the Roman army, who had no inhibitions about being dressed in full military panoply at their funerals.

Usually their nationality can only be identified from the neighbouring graves of their wives with their distinctive 'folk costume' dress fasteners. In the case of those Lankhills graves which occur in a sector of the cemetery coin-dated to the second half of the fourth century, it seems likely that these soldiers and their families were Sarmatians, a nomadic horse people from the steppes. Presumably they had been recruited in the Hungarian plain east of the Danube frontier at Budapest (*Acquincum*). On the other hand, the excavator's claim that another group of foreigners buried at Lankhills between *c*.390 and 410 were Saxons can be dismissed in the absence of any north German object among either the male or the female graves there.

The withdrawal of most of the Roman army from Britain by 407 to campaign in Gaul and Spain was followed by the failure of the Emperor Honorius to appoint new governors to the provinces of Britain around 410, let alone send troops to help his British subjects defend themselves from an attack by the Saxons. A few Roman troops may have been left behind to provide a skeleton garrison for some of the forts along Hadrian's Wall and perhaps a few on the coastal defences as well. If so, in all probability they did not receive any pay after 407 and almost certainly they would have had to turn to farming to feed themselves and their families. Over a few generations they will have lost much of their military character and disci-pline, gradually merging into the local popu-lation. There is no evidence that any of the Roman generals operating across the Channel in northern Gaul up to the 480s actually attempted to mount a military expedition to recover Britain for the Empire. Gildas mentions that some Britons contacted Aëtius, requesting his intervention, but he faced enough problems in the 440s and 450s trying to control both Gaul and Italy.

Saxon mercenaries

The rulers of Britain after 410 are referred to as 'tyrants' because their authority had no legitimacy in Roman eyes. They probably feared a Roman invasion from Gaul to remove them. According to Gildas, a proud tyrant hired Saxons to fight for him and settled them in the eastern part of the island. The major threat being anticipated seems to have been a Pictish invasion from northern Scotland, possibly by sea down the east coast, for the Picts are described in one Late Roman source as a sea-going people. It would make sense to use another seafaring people, the Saxons, to counter this threat. If some of these Saxons were stationed in Kent, then they may have had an additional role to guard against any Roman military intervention from Gaul during this emergency.

It may be that we can both identify and date the graves of some warriors who might have been among those Saxons hired by that British ruler. These men were buried wearing Late Roman official belt sets and accompanied by weapons and are among the earliest datable graves in newly-founded Anglo-Saxon cemeter-ies such as the second cemetery at Mucking. Presumably they had gained their military training and expertise from service in the Roman army on the Continent. Their belt sets and other equipment can be dated from Roman coins found in weapon graves in Gaul and along the Rhine frontier. A recent reassessment of this continental cemetery evidence by a Ger-man archaeologist suggests that the earliest types of Roman belt equipment found in Anglo-Saxon cemeteries in England belong rather later than used to be thought.

For example, it was once normal to date the belt set discovered in 1874 at a grave by the Dyke Hills near Dorchester-on-Thames to around 400 (see **71**). It is now clear that it belongs to a type broadly datable to the middle third of the fifth century in Gaul. This man, equipped as if he was, or had once been, a Roman officer, no longer needs to die and be buried before the Roman army is transported to Gaul in 407. Burial in the 430s or the 440s seems more probable. If the female grave found nearby belongs to his wife or a female relation, then it is likely that he was a Saxon from north Germany. Her brooches certainly come from that region. There is an early simple type of cruciform brooch, a disc brooch which has lost its decorated top plate, as well as a locally-made Romano-British buckle for a narrow and probably non-official leather belt (**72**).

Neither burial would have looked out of place in a contemporary Saxon cemetery in north Germany between the rivers Weser and Elbe and it may well be that they formed part of an otherwise unexplored Anglo-Saxon cemetery to the south-west of the small Roman town at Dorchester. A belt and weapon assem-blage excavated in 1957 at Liebenau near the

72 *North German brooches and a small Romano-British belt buckle and plate from a woman's grave by the Dorchester Dyke Hills.*

Weser gives us an idea of the range of iron weapons which the Dorchester workmen of 1874 threw away as worthless into the Thames river from the man's grave. Unfortunately the present landowner is unwilling to allow archaeological excavation to reinvestigate this important site.

Not all the weapon burials can be clearly categorized as either 'foreign' troops in Late Roman cemeteries, who probably left Britain by 407, or else Saxon mercenaries hired by an independent British ruler rather later in the first half of the fifth century. A burial with a spear and shield of north German type and a Roman pewter bowl was accidentally discovered a short distance from the Richborough (*Rutupiae*) Saxon Shore fort (Kent) in the late 1920s or 1930s (**73**). As a similar shield boss was

recovered from an inner fort ditch, he was presumably a member of the garrison. Unfortunately we cannot date these objects closely though they belong within the first half of the fifth century. As a result we cannot decide whether he was a member of the last regular army garrison of the first decade of that century, or whether he was a Saxon mercenary stationed there decades later by the British authorities to defend the Kentish coast from Pictish or Roman attack.

Until there are funds to mount a thorough archaeological exploration of the garrison cemeteries at Richborough, this ambiguity will remain. A similar fort cemetery was excavated on the Belgian coast at Oudenburg in 1963-4, producing a valuable group of coin-dated graves of men recruited from east of the Rhine frontier. Once again they were accompanied by wives and families. Such discoveries on the Continent make it clear that we are never going to understand what happened to the last garrisons of the Roman forts in Britain if we only excavate the forts themselves and do not thoroughly investigate their extramural cemeteries.

So to summarize, the archaeological evidence that has been used to justify the claim that significant numbers of Anglo-Saxons were settled in eastern Britain before 400 fails to stand up to close examination. There may have been Roman troops recruited from north Germany or south Scandinavia stationed in Britain in the first decade of the fifth century. If so, these Anglo-Saxons will represent just one of the many barbarian nationalities present in the Roman army here. Probably most, if not all of them, will have been transferred across the Channel to Gaul by 407.

The men buried with weapons and Roman belt sets in Anglo-Saxon cemeteries seem to have arrived here at least two decades after 407, though still within the first half of the fifth century. It is tempting to see such warrior burials as the graves of Saxon mercenaries hired by the British 'proud tyrants', who then successfully rebelled and carved out small kingdoms for themselves in east and south-east England. Other possibilities are that some Anglo-Saxons were allowed by the British to settle in depopulated areas without playing any significant military role, or else took advantage of British disunity to invade and seize territory.

By the 420s or 430s Roman wheelthrown

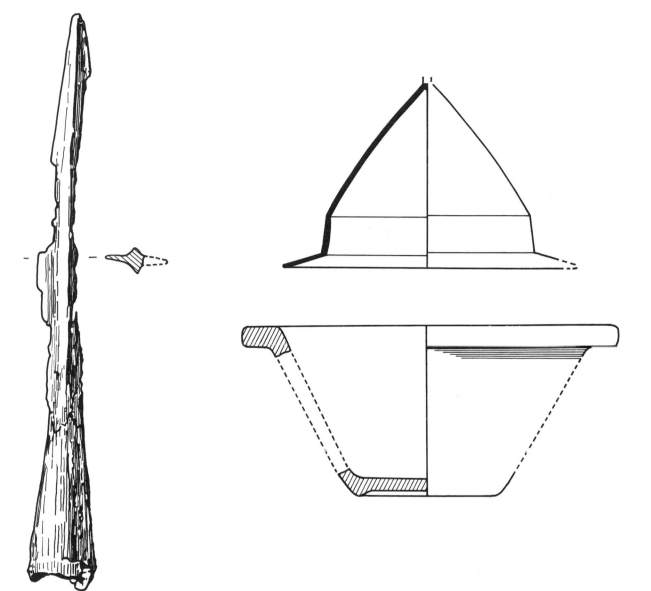

pottery was no longer being manuufactured or distributed in Britain. If it had been available to the earliest Anglo-Saxon settlers, we can be reasonably sure that they would have been buried with Roman pots. Equivalent graves of fifth-century Frankish warriors and their wives in Gaul always include several Roman vessels, often glass or metal containers as well as pottery. But then most of the major Roman industries in Gaul continued in production without any significant break through the fifth century and on into the sixth and seventh centuries. Unfortunately we cannot date the

73 *Spearhead, shield boss and pewter bowl recovered with a burial near the Richborough (Kent) Saxon Shore fort.*

end of wheelthrown pottery in Britain with any precision. It coincides with and is quite possibly associated with the end of large-scale import of Roman coins from imperial mints to Britain c.402 to pay the army and civil service.

Continuity or discontinuity?

It has been claimed that the presence of Anglo-Saxon *Grubenhäuser* in various towns such as Canterbury (Kent) and Colchester (Essex) provide evidence for continuity of urban occupation. On the other hand, some Roman towns were deserted and never reoccupied, for example Silchester (Hampshire) and *Verulamium* near St Albans (Hertfordshire). All towns in Roman Britain seem to have been in decline in terms of their habitation area and population size from the third century onwards. It is not clear that any of them really deserved to be called a town after the first decade of the fifth century. Deposits of black earth, partly derived from accumulated wind-blown rubbish, built up within the walls of many towns between the late third and seventh centuries.

These deposits surely reflect neglect and abandonment. At best there may have been a limited squatter occupation between ruined walls and collapsing roofs at the time the Anglo-Saxons took control of a town like Canterbury (**colour plate 6**).

The small settlements constructed by the Anglo-Saxons within their walled circuits in the fifth, sixth and seventh centuries may have been essentially the same as their equivalents in the open countryside. Perhaps they exploited the cultivation potential of the rich organic black earth within former towns. Much the same can be argued for the fifth-century and later Anglo-Saxon occupation of the Roman fort at Portchester Castle overlooking Portsmouth Harbour. Certainly there seems to have been a long gap between its abandonment by a regular army garrison in the later fourth century and a limited Anglo-Saxon settlement which may be no earlier than the middle decades of the fifth century.

If by continuity we mean the survival of Roman provincial administration, religious institutions and Latin, then there is no such continuity in Anglo-Saxon England. By contrast, in France, Spain and Italy, Christian bishops flourished in Roman towns which survived as urban centres and Romance languages based on Latin eventually triumphed over the Germanic languages of the Franks, Burgundians and Goths. The organization of the Church had to be rebuilt from scratch in England by missionaries from Rome and Frankish Gaul in the seventh century. Admittedly former Roman town sites were favoured by Italian and French missionaries for episcopal sees, but a significant number of bishoprics were based in rural centres, as at Selsey in Sussex, despite the

presence of nearby Roman Chichester. There is no suggestion that any of these towns survived as more than shadows of their former selves, though there may have been some impressive ruins still standing (**colour plate 7**).

Bede claimed that before Augustine's mission arrived, the Christian Frankish princess married to the pagan Æthelberht of Kent used a Roman stone building east of Canterbury for her private chapel. The parish church of St Martin almost certainly incorporates this chapel and may have adapted a Roman mausoleum. This suggests that her residence was nearby on the same hill and not within the town walls of Canterbury. We have no reason to believe that there was a royal palace in the Roman town prior to the Christian mission.

Traces of Anglo-Saxon timber buildings and burials have also been excavated on the sites of a number of Roman villas. Where the Anglo-Saxon structures or graves can be dated, they as often prove to belong to the sixth or seventh centuries, as to the fifth century. In most cases we can suspect that the villa itself had been deserted long before the arrival and settlement of an Anglo-Saxon farming community there. Rather than taking over a complete and intact working farm estate, it may be that the Anglo-Saxons simply chose to live there because they wanted to be adjacent to the best agricultural land in the area.

A small number of cases have been put forward which have been thought to show the continuity of a Roman villa and its estate, the most famous being at Withington (Gloucestershire). An estate was granted there for the foundation of a monastery and was recorded in eighth-century charters. The fact that the boundaries of the Anglo-Saxon estate match those we would expect for the Roman villa estate proves nothing. Geographical determinism should not be allowed to disguise the fact that as we have no Roman documents listing the boundaries of the Withington villa, we do not know what land belonged to that villa.

Wasperton

Possible continuity of a different sort has been claimed recently at Wasperton in the Avon valley between Stratford-on-Avon and Warwick (**74**). A small Late Roman cemetery there produced a significant number of late fifth- to seventh-century Anglo-Saxon graves. Could this represent a British community, which by

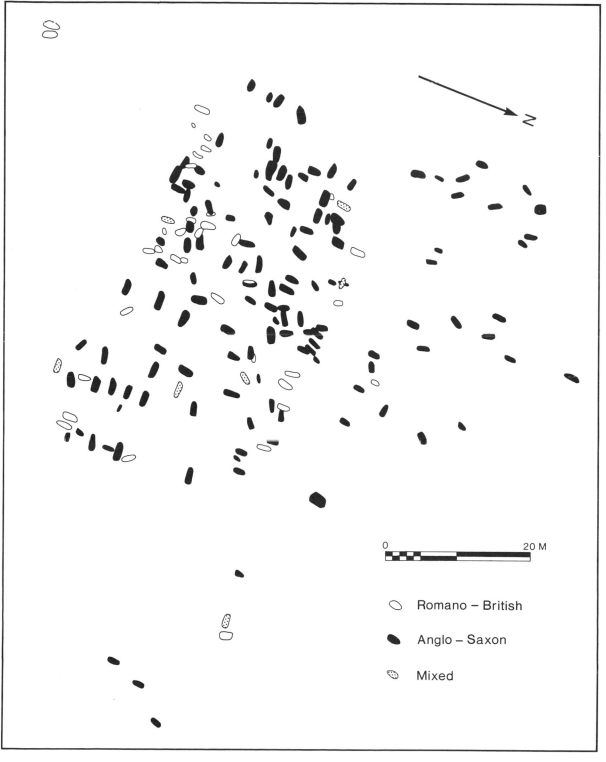

74 *Plan of the Late Roman and Anglo-Saxon burial ground at Wasperton (Warwicks.).*

the late fifth century had adopted Anglo-Saxon burial customs and dress fashions from their new political masters? Alternatively, it may be that newly-arrived Anglo-Saxon settlers recognized and adopted an abandoned Romano-British grave field for their own use before the end of the fifth century. Only initial reports have been published for this excavation, but fuller analysis may yet provide conclusive evidence one way or the other.

It has been claimed that 17 inhumations and one cremation had Roman characteristics, such as distinctive metal fittings, hobnail boots or ritual mutilation of the corpse, including decapitation. There were also 82 inhumations accompanied by Anglo-Saxon objects and 20 Anglo-Saxon cremations. Grave orientation also helps to differentiate between the Romano-British burials, which were N-S with a few E-W and the Anglo-Saxons, who were placed S-N and W-E. Some of the Anglo-Saxon graves had disturbed earlier burials on a different alignment. On the basis of orientation, the total of Romano-British burials can be raised to 47,

75 *A co-axial field system in the area of Scole and Dickleburgh (Norfolk).*

and there were 124 Anglo-Saxon inhumations. In fact 101 of the 200 excavated burials contained no finds, or else objects which did not assist in identifying the date of their deposition. These form about 50 per cent of the total cemetery, but to argue that most of the undatable burials belong to the fifth century and link the definite Late Roman graves to the Anglo-Saxon burials may be wishful thinking.

The landscape

Real continuity of settlement and community, as opposed to Anglo-Saxon reuse of abandoned Roman settlements and exploitation of their fields, has therefore proved extremely difficult for the archaeologist to demonstrate in practice. Yet pollen analysis does not indicate any great ecological change in this transition period, as there is no evidence for large-scale abandonment of farmland and no accompanying regeneration and expansion of woodland. If by continuity we mean that there was no time in the fifth and sixth centuries when the landscape of lowland Britain ceased to be inhabited, ploughed, pastured or otherwise exploited by human society, then surely there was continuity. The problem is how to show that this was the case.

We can suspect, but not easily prove, that many British peasant farmers were reluctant to abandon their landholdings. They may well have proved willing to reach an arrangement with their new political masters, the Anglo-Saxons, providing they were allowed to stay. This is not to say that there was no bloodshed or upheaval involved, merely that we can exaggerate its effects. It is no more than an impression, which is difficult to quantify, but there does seem to have been a drastic fall in the rural population during the late fourth and fifth centuries. The individuals buried in Anglo-Saxon cemeteries do not seem to have suffered much from malnutrition and appear to occupy a relatively empty landscape. For example, Roman drainage schemes which permitted low-lying land to be farmed near the Thames in the Abingdon region were allowed to silt up through lack of maintenance. Perhaps it was sufficient to exploit this land as water meadow again and it may be that much Roman plough-land was turned over to pasture in this period.

There is a working assumption that Late Roman field systems were acquired and farmed by Anglo-Saxon settlers, though relatively little archaeological work has been carried out to demonstrate this hypothesis. These field systems need not be limited to the lighter loamy soils favoured by prehistoric farmers and still popular with Early Anglo-Saxon settlers, if the distribution of known Anglo-Saxon cemeteries and settlements means anything. For example, early co-axial field boundaries can be traced on heavy clay soil in the Scole-Dickleburgh area of south Norfolk. Because a Roman road diagonally crosses this field system, as if the fields were not there, it has been suggested that these small rectangular fields were probably pre-Roman in origin. An alternative possibility is that the co-axial fields here were created later within the Anglo-Saxon period, after this particular road went out of use (**75**).

Some Anglo-Saxon kingdoms preserved a Roman or British regional name: Kent (from *Cantiaci*) and Deira in Yorkshire are good examples. In such cases we can suspect that the Anglo-Saxons took over more or less intact the existing administrative organization of the rural landscape in that region. The regions called 'lathes' in Kent may have their origins in pre-Roman and Roman rural districts and the system of food rents and labour services based on them may have been adopted without any major changes by the Anglo-Saxons who took over Kent in the fifth century. We should bear in mind, however, that the system of agriculture practised by the Anglo-Saxons in north Germany and south Scandinavia was not radically different from that of the Romano-British peasantry. The British estate organization of the landscape may not have seemed particularly alien to them. Indeed the Anglo-Saxons may well have adapted it to suit their needs. Certainly the names of the royal settlement centres for the lathes, the Kentish equivalents of Yeavering, survive in English forms. Often they end in *-ge*, a word related to modern German *Gau*, meaning a district or region. Thus Eastry (*Easterege*) was the 'capital' of the eastern district and Lyminge its equivalent for a district based on the river Lympne. Significantly the district named after the river Stour, which flows through Canterbury, was not based in the Roman town, but at Sturry just a few miles further downstream. Anglo-Saxon Kent in the early seventh century was essentially a rural society.

9

Manufacture and trade

Even with the combined information of finds recovered from both settlement and burial sites, the archaeological evidence for manufacture and trade between the fifth and seventh centuries is far from complete. Perishable agricultural products and items manufactured from organic materials (e.g. wood or animal bone) generally do not survive in a recognizable form in the soil. The detection of organic residues through chemical tests is unfortunately an expensive and time-consuming business.

Occasionally special conditions preserve evidence, as with grain that has become charred by fire, or textile thread protected by adjacent metal objects when buried. Even then care must be taken in interpretation. For example, loose reject grain might well be placed in a bread oven to stop the bread being baked from sticking to the clay surfaces of the oven. It is this disposable grain which is likely to become charred, yet this tells us nothing about the grain used to make the bread.

Nor can we make much use of written sources, though we can note that slaves were frequently mentioned as exports to the Continent. It was Pope Gregory's discovery of pagan Anglian slaves on sale at Rome which inspired him to organize Augustine's mission to Kent. Unfortunately slavery has left no obvious trace in the archaeological record.

The range of craft activities
Excavation of settlements tells us something about the everyday tasks which every community would undertake. Quernstones were needed to grind grain. Imported lava from the Niedermendig region of the Rhineland was a favoured material for this, being light. Thirteen *Grubenhäuser* at West Stow contained lava

quernstone fragments, while millstones made from the same material were recovered from an excavated ninth-century horizontal water mill at Tamworth (Staffordshire) (**76**). A surviving letter from Charlemagne to Offa in 796 tells us that the Frankish ruler was sending the 'black stones' requested by the Mercian king. As Tamworth was an important Mercian royal centre, this mill may well have been owned by one of Offa's successors. But we have no idea how the West Stow community and others like it set about acquiring lava quernstones. It is difficult to believe that they relied solely on acquiring stones from deserted Roman sites.

Spinning wool and weaving cloth on upright looms was another common activity revealed by the presence of spindlewhorls and clay loomweights in many sunken featured buildings. Traces of metalworking also seem to imply that basic smithing skills were available in most rural communities. These could involve tasks such as simple repairs to splits in wooden vessels using bronze riveted clips, or forging an iron edge and fixing it to a wooden spade or plough. As yet though, no proper ironworking smithy area has been excavated from any settlement earlier than the eighth century. Normally all that is found at settlements like Mucking is redeposited debris from a smithy, but no trace of the smithy itself.

Simple lathes used to turn wooden bowls leave no trace, nor usually do the finished and unfinished turned wooden vessels. Only if the exceptional preservation conditions of Feddersen Wierde can be repeated in an English waterlogged site, could we hope to recover a wood-turner's or a wheel-wright's workshop. At least we have learnt to recognize metal repairs to wooden bowls and to see the dark

1. Shaft
2. Millstone
3. Hopper
4. Scooping up the flour

stains which they can leave in a grave. It is now clear that wooden vessels must have formed an important part of Early Anglo-Saxon household inventories.

Pottery production

Another basic container, the clay pot, also appears to have been produced on a domestic household basis in most communities. Dumps of clay, probably collected for potting, have been recognized at the settlements of West Stow and Sutton Courtenay. Antler stamps for decorating pots have also been recovered at a number of sites. Yet once again the actual process of manufacture leaves little trace. A simple kiln excavated at Cassington (Oxfordshire) was once attributed to an Early Anglo-Saxon potter, on the basis of a few sherds of

76 *Reconstruction of the ninth-century watermill excavated at Tamworth (Staffs.) whose powered wheel was set horizontally. This technology can still be found on Crete. (The Trustees of the British Museum.)*

handmade pottery in it, but it seems more probable now that this evidence was misunderstood. Instead the low-temperature and uneven firing achieved on typical finished products seem to result from building nothing more elaborate than a bonfire over a stack of sun-dried leather-hard pots.

The range of forms and decoration of Anglo-Saxon handmade pots is relatively limited and seems to be bound by traditional practices. In those societies which still build their clay vessels without a potter's wheel, it is often

109

women who make pots. If this was also the case in Anglo-Saxon England, then a mother (or aunt) might teach her daughters (nieces) the correct way to make pottery, handed down from generation to generation in a family tradition. Each pot she or her pupils produced would be both unique and yet still linked to the others by obedience to rules for shaping the vessel and applying ornament to it. In time, each daughter might add her own personal contribution within this framework: her distinguishing mark.

That such an interpretation is not completely fanciful can be suggested by examining pots which share a limited range of stamp designs in their ornamentation, implying perhaps that they could be the work of a single producer. Stamp-linked pots have been identified within individual cemeteries, but can also recur in several cemeteries, providing an unambiguous link between the pots in them. Even within a large and systematically-excavated urnfield, however, each stamped-linked group present actually represents a relatively small number of pots (for instance, Spong Hill Group 7/12 with 31 pots is the largest grouping in that cemetery, see **59**).

Other stamped-linked groups occur across several cremation cemeteries within a relatively compact region, as with the Illington-Lackford group on the Norfolk-Suffolk borders (**77**). All these cemeteries are within a 48km (30 mile) radius. It has been suggested that this was the maximum distance customers would walk to market in order to purchase Illington-Lackford pots in the sixth century. If so, how are we to explain other stamp-linked pot groups which are much more widely distributed, such as the Sancton-Baston pots. These occur in dispersed sites between the Yorkshire Wolds (Sancton), the Trent valley (Newark) and Norfolk (Illington). Coastal and river craft would provide the most obvious means of linking all these communities (**78**).

Study of pottery fabric within such groups has only complicated matters still further. This indicates that a variety of clay sources were being exploited. Far from showing that all the pots in a stamp-linked group were made in a single workshop, this implies instead dispersed production. It seems a mistake to think of any of these pots as products of a commercial operation; they are unlikely to have been made by specialist potters for sale or barter.

77 *A sixth-century pot of the Illington-Lackford stamp group.*

If we see this pottery as produced on an essentially domestic scale by women, the distribution patterns become easier to understand. Each daughter could have taken copies of her mother's stamps to her husband's settlement on marriage. She would have in her head the traditional 'template', which governed how she made and decorated her pots. To this she might add her own personal contribution. The same type of pot with matching, or at least similar decoration, but using the various local clays, can appear in as many cemeteries (or settlements) as there were daughters eligible to be married off.

This is not to say that pots were never traded. Certainly some wheelthrown pottery was imported from the Frankish regions of northeast France and Belgium to Anglo-Saxon England from the late sixth and seventh centuries onwards. The bulk of these are restricted to Kent and Essex. It is debatable though, whether any of this pottery was brought over in its own right. Rather it could be seen as an indicator of trade in another commodity. There are more serving bottles, jugs and pitchers than anything else among the imports from Kentish inhumations. Perhaps they had been offered as 'free gifts' with each barrel of French wine purchased, used as sale inducements like glasses at petrol stations.

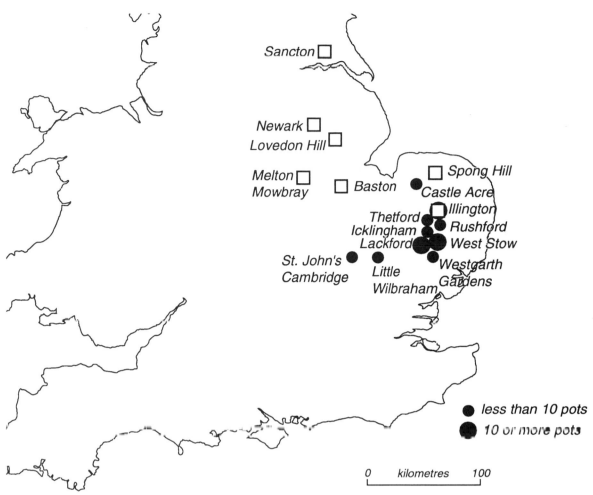

Illington - Lackford pottery stamp group ● *and Sancton-Baston group* □

Sancton □

Newark □
Lovedon Hill □

Melton □
Mowbray

□ Baston

□ Spong Hill

● Castle Acre

□ Illington

Thetford
Icklingham
Lackford

● Rushford

West Stow

St. John's ●
Cambridge

Little
Wilbraham

Westgarth
Gardens

● *less than 10 pots*

● *10 or more pots*

0   kilometres   100

78 *Distribution map comparing the Illington-Lackford pottery stamp group to the more dispersed Sancton-Baston pottery stamp group.*

Metalworking

Turning to more sophisticated levels of manufacture, it is unfortunate that we lack a single site with well-preserved debris from metalworking workshops producing dress fastenings and jewellery. It is not as if metal manufacturing evidence is unknown from the British Isles and Ireland as a whole for this period. Evidence for metal and glass working have been recovered by excavation from what seem to be 'princely' centres. Examples are the small hillfort at Dinas Powys near Cardiff and the Mote of Mark in south-west Scotland, as well as numerous Early Christian period Irish sites. Some moulds from Yeavering are to be published shortly and other high-status settlements of Yeavering type may reveal workshop evidence for Anglo-Saxon England in the future, but few

of these have been excavated as yet.

The rich evidence recovered by excavation between the 1950s and 1970s on the small island of Helgö on Lake Mälaren near Stockholm (Sweden) shows what might yet be found here. Large dumps of fragmentary clay moulds used for casting a wide range of sixth-century metalwork were revealed. There were also the clay crucibles and the hearth pits in which those crucibles were heated to produce molten silver or bronze for casting, as well as many iron tools. More recent, but still unpublished discoveries in Sweden indicate that manufacturing sites of a similar type to those on Helgö

111

were fairly common in the Mälaren region.

Evidence from England is limited to fragments of a single brooch mould from a sunken featured building at Mucking. At least this demonstrates that the method of casting manufacture used in sixth-century England was the same as that known from Scandinavia. It is possible that more careful examination of all the clay material excavated at Mucking might have revealed further evidence for a metal workshop there, as much of it was simply dumped by the excavators. This makes it essential that future settlement excavations pay special attention to any potential evidence for metalworking and indeed all craft activity.

Smith graves

More surprising still has been the almost complete absence in Anglo-Saxon cemeteries of smith graves containing metalworking tools and scrap for reuse as cast metal. These are an important, though hardly a common feature of the cemetery evidence on the mainland of Europe. An example is the assemblage containing a shield as well as iron tools, including hammers, a small anvil and a whetstone, from Poysdorf Grave 6 in Austria.

This burial also contained two bronze 'models' of sixth-century brooches (**79**). These

79 Brooch models from a smith grave at Poysdorf (Austria).

'models' lack the pin-fittings or gilding of finished brooches, but it seems unlikely that they are just partly-finished items. Complete versions of these brooches in local cemeteries were always cast in silver and then gilded. What we have here are cheap metal prototypes. These could be used to produce clay moulds, from which silver duplicates could then be cast. Presumably they were placed in the grave to symbolize the smith's skill in casting jewellery as well as working other metals.

Similar metal 'models' for brooches in either bronze or lead have been recovered from settlement sites on the Continent. It has been claimed that one such model for an Anglo-Saxon saucer brooch was excavated at Cassington, but this item has since been mislaid, so the claim cannot be checked. From such evidence the concept of itinerant metalsmiths has been developed. It has proved to be an attractive theory, for it seems to explain the geographical distribution of finished brooches in grave assemblages.

Clearly the community represented by the small cemetery at Poysdorf could not supply enough work for the master smith buried there. So perhaps he travelled in a circuit from settlement to settlement, showing his complete set of brooch and other 'models' at each as samples. He might take orders to reproduce them in a temporary workshop set up then and there. Perhaps he was accompanied by assistants or apprentices. Presumably he would need to

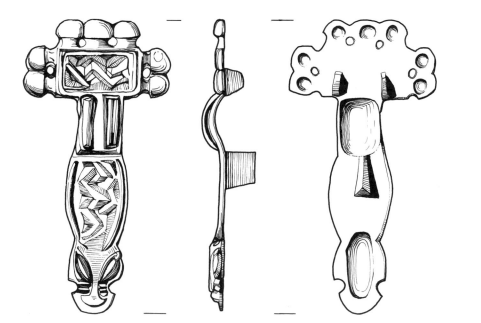

Square - headed brooches (group VII)

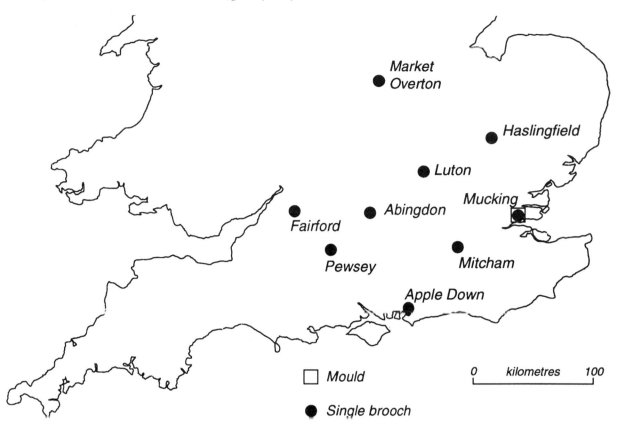

80 *Distribution map of Group VII square-headed brooches.*

transport some quantities of precious metals, whether using pack animals or a cart, and perhaps he had a small bodyguard to protect against armed robbery. Alternatively his clients may have been expected to produce much of the metal themselves. Old or broken brooches could be recycled by his skill into the latest fashions.

A sealed capsule containing droplets of mercury associated with iron tools in a smith's grave at Hérouvillette near Caen (France) might well be linked to fire-gilding. In this process, thin gold sheet or paste is applied with mercury to the surface of the object to be gilded. Heating the other side of the object drives off the mercury and binds the gold firmly to the surface. A bronze or silver brooch or buckle is thus given the superficial appearance of a solid gold item. Mercury poisoning must have been one of the working hazards.

The Helgö evidence, however, suggests a different mode of organization to the wandering smith. Instead, the workshop and the craftsmen themselves are permanently based in one place. Indeed the metalworkers may have been primarily farmers, who practised their craft during gaps in the farming year. Did they send out salesmen armed with sets of samples, perhaps 'models', to collect orders which would be delivered later that year? Or did these craftsmen speculate, producing a stock of brooches and other dress fastenings ready for sale? Were there markets at particular places on a given day, week or month, at which they could barter their products? We cannot yet begin to answer such questions for central Sweden, but that should not stop us posing the same questions for Early Anglo-Saxon England.

On balance, the concept of semi-permanent workshops as the basis for the production of standard dress fittings in fifth- and sixth-century England seems as probable as the itinerant smith explanation. Regional studies

113

Square - headed brooches (group XVI)

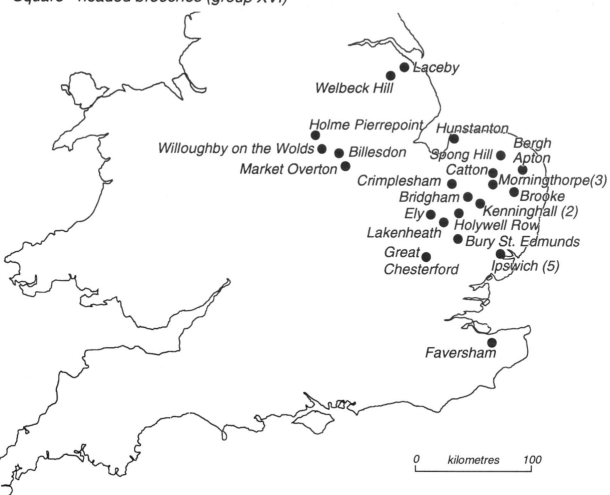

81 *Distribution map of Group XVI square-headed brooches presumably manufactured in East Anglia.*

of Anglo-Saxon cemeteries over the last twenty years have helped to clarify the distribution patterns of particular brooch types (**80** and **81**). For example, they allow us to distinguish between saucer brooches which seem to have been produced in the Lower Thames valley and those typical of the Upper Thames region around Oxford (**82**). Women taking their brooches with them when they married may explain their presence in cemeteries well away from the Thames valley. In any case we can define a core distribution area of finished products. We can go on to suggest a region, within which either itinerant smiths were circulating,

or there existed more permanent metalworking centres. But as yet, we cannot locate the physical remains of the workshops themselves in these regions.

A rather different type of 'model', this time cast in bronze, has been recovered from a number of sites in England. These are dies ornamented with seventh-century animal art designs and used to apply those designs on to sheets of bronze, silver or gold. Thin hammered foils were placed over the dies and rubbed down over them: a type of ornament known as *repoussé*. They were used to decorate mounts on buckets, drinking horns, wooden cups and a host of other objects.

Two *repoussé* rectangular dies or 'models' were excavated in the late nineteenth century from a cemetery at Icklingham (Suffolk) (**83**),

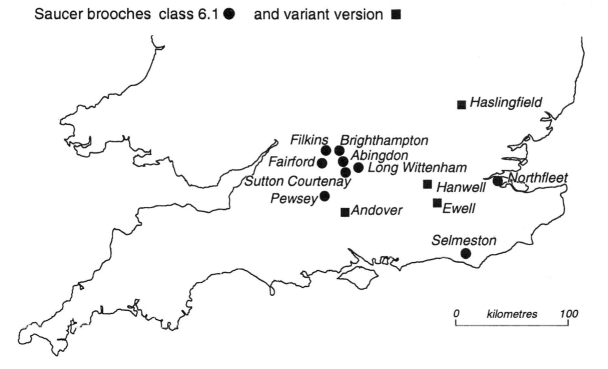

Saucer brooches class 6.1 ● and variant version ■

Filkins
Brighthampton
Fairford
Abingdon
Sutton Courtenay
Long Wittenham
Pewsey
Andover
Haslingfield
Hanwell
Northfleet
Ewell
Selmeston

0 kilometres 100

82 *Distribution map of two versions of a sixth-century saucer brooch design: both probably manufactured in the Thames Valley region.*

not far from West Stow. Another disc-shaped die was found in 1939 in a grave at Barton-on-Humber (South Humberside). It had been reused as a weight with a pair of balances or scales. The most recent published find was recovered from a medieval rubbish pit in Rochester (Kent). It is basically rectangular, but has a marked curvature making it especially suitable for producing mounts to be fitted on to the rim of a small drinking vessel.

Die-links from finished items of *repoussé*-decorated metalwork can be very informative. The use of the same dies to make drinking horn mounts from both mounds 1 and 2 at Sutton Hoo has already been mentioned. This means that the coin-dating evidence from mound 1 can be applied to all the objects recovered from the robbed mound 2 grave. In turn, this makes the blue glass vase from mound 2 a key dated item, helping us to estimate dates of manufacture for this distinctive glass type.

A fascinating discovery was made by chance during a recent rescue excavation near Tattershall Thorpe in Lincolnshire. It seems to be the first convincing example of a smith's grave in Anglo-Saxon England. Unfortunately it seems to have been an isolated inhumation burial, rather than belonging to a cemetery. Part of a

83 *Bronze dies with seventh-century animal designs for producing* repoussé *ornament from Icklingham (Suffolk). (Dr G. Speake.)*

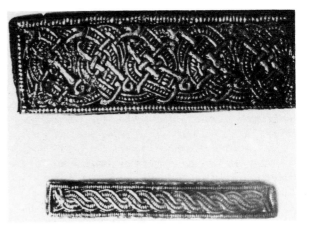

115

blue glass vase among glass fragments suggests a date in the seventh century. It also contained a variety of iron tools and anvils as well as several neat rectangular cloth packets filled with scrap items of bronze. The future publication of this exciting large assemblage will mark an important milestone in the development of our understanding of the equipment and skills of Anglo-Saxon metalworkers.

Balances in graves

Graves containing balances have often been singled out as belonging to smiths or merchants. Certainly the ability to weigh metal bullion accurately would be valuable to both smiths and merchants, but this need not be what their presence symbolized in Anglo-Saxon graves. The distribution of graves with pairs of balances in western Europe has been contrasted with the distribution of coin mints documented for the seventh-century Frankish kingdoms. While there is a certain degree of overlap, graves with balances are predominantly found in the German Rhineland and east of that river. Balances represent a necessary mechanism for assessing the value of gold and silver coins in territories which did not mint their own coins. Their populations were not used to accepting coins without first weighing them. West of the Rhine, within the former frontiers of the Roman Empire, coins were more likely to be accepted at their face-value.

Anglo-Saxon England in the sixth and for much of the seventh century was similarly a region without coinage of its own and bullion will have been valued on the basis of weight. Roman coinage had ceased to enter the British provinces in bulk c.402. By the 420s, if not earlier, the existing coin stock of Roman Britain had surely ceased to function as a money economy. The importation of relatively small quantities of coinage from the Frankish kingdoms during the first half of the seventh century and the imitation of Roman and Frankish coin designs in early attempts to mint coins in southeast England during the seventh century mark the first faltering steps towards the issue of coins there.

Those individuals buried with pairs of balances need not be moneyers, smiths or merchants. They might equally well be royal officials charged with exacting tolls from merchants at market places, and overseeing the payment of fines by coin or bullion for penalties described in the seventh-century Kentish law codes. Perhaps they also supervised the payments made in compensation settlements for death or injury (*wergild*), provided the family of the injured party agreed. These prevented, or at least limited, the impact of feuds between kin groups.

Glass working

There is some indirect evidence to suggest that craftsmen in Kent were capable of producing glass vessels in quantity during the sixth and seventh centuries and even exported some to the Continent or to Scandinavia. This is based on the fact that certain types of vessel, which are relatively common in Kentish graves, are rare finds in continental burials. The distribution patterns of squat jars, bag-beakers, pouch-bottles and some types of claw-beaker can be read in this way. We know that Kentish workshops were capable of making remarkable jewellery, with masterpieces such as the Kingston and Amherst composite disc brooches, which are finer than any equivalent disc brooches produced in mainland Europe at that date.

Yet this evidence for glass vessel production is perhaps suspect and differences in burial practice between south-east England and the Frankish Continent may provide the real explanation. Of course, the same objection can be raised whenever we are reliant on the distribution of finished products from cemeteries and lack archaeological evidence for manufacture. There are still no known production sites to demonstrate conclusively glass vessel manufacture in Kent in this period.

Trade networks

The raw materials for the finest jewellery had to be imported. Garnets may have been brought from as far as India and Ceylon in the sixth and seventh centuries, and amethyst from the east Mediterranean region or even India in the seventh century. Gold was normally obtained by melting down imported coins. As Frankish gold coins were progressively devalued by the addition of ever larger proportions of silver during the first half of the seventh century, so the metal of contemporary Anglo-Saxon gold ornaments became visibly paler and paler.

The seventh-century devaluation of Frankish coinage reflected a wider shortage of gold, which was no longer freely available from the East Roman Empire. Then when the sources of plate garnet dried up towards the middle of the seventh century, Anglo Saxon jewellers were forced to recut garnets from old jewellery, and both the garnets and their settings became smaller and smaller. By the second half of the seventh century only much larger, better quality and therefore more expensive garnet stones were still being imported. These were now placed individually as polished *cabochon* settings in pendants (**colour plate 4**). Imported

84 *Distribution of 'Coptic' cast bronze vessels from graves from Italy to south-east England illustrating a trade route using Alpine passes and the Rhine valley to bring Mediterranean products to Kent and East Anglia in the sixth to seventh centuries.*

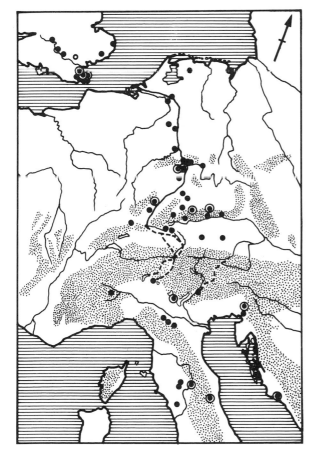

● 1 Coptic bronze vessel

◉ 2 – 4 Coptic bronze vessels

amethysts were also now set in this way, as were some items of finely decorated glass.

Distribution maps based on finished objects, mainly recovered from burials, make it clear that Kent represented one end of a major trade route utilizing the Rhine valley and the Swiss Alpine passes. This linked north-west Europe to Italy, the Adriatic Sea and the East Mediterranean beyond. Cast bronze containers, often referred to as Coptic vessels, are one of the principal markers of this route (**84**). They have been found in a significant number of Kentish graves and in many of the 'princely' burials of south-east England, including Sutton Hoo. These burial contexts date them to the late sixth and early seventh centuries. Such vessels were not necessarily all made in Coptic (Christian) Egypt, for other centres in the Eastern Roman Empire seem to have been producing similar containers.

Other river and road networks from the Mediterranean ports across what is now France may have contributed to the trading network which could bring garnets and amethysts to Kent, as well as cowrie shells from the Red Sea. Simple cast and sheet-made bronze bowls, together with a wide variety of glass vessels, all of which appear to be the products of fifth- to seventh-century workshops in the Meuse and Rhine regions, do seem to confirm the importance of the Rhine routeway, as do rock crystal and lava querns mined in Rhineland quarries.

Not all these imports were to leave Kent in any quantity to be traded to other parts of Anglo-Saxon England. For example, very few rock crystal balls have been found outside Kent, whereas smaller beads of rock crystal are widely distributed across England in the sixth century. Similarly, gold-thread embroidered headbands worn by women in the sixth century, or late sixth- and seventh-century Frankish wheelmade vessels are rare finds outside Kent.

Control of imported luxury goods may have been an important diplomatic weapon for the kings of Kent. They could reward their allies and followers with gifts of these luxuries, while withholding them from those who had incurred displeasure. Large and elaborate gifts of luxury goods inevitably place the recipient in the debt of the giver. It may well be that the Kentish rulers were acting as proxy agents for Merovingian Frankish kings who appear to have claimed overlordship over southern England in the sixth century. It was apparently the Franks and their Kentish subordinates then who controlled access to the status symbols prized by members of the Anglo-Saxon élites.

Trading settlements

We have not yet located the Kentish ports through which both imports and exports were unloaded and loaded. An interesting suggestion has been made that the cemeteries at Sarre on Thanet, and Buckland, Dover, contain relatively large numbers of sword burials because these represent the warbands of the king's port-reeves there. Unfortunately no direct evidence for a sixth- or seventh-century port has been traced at Sarre or Dover. By the middle of the seventh century written sources imply that Sandwich was a port for cross-Channel shipping and the same can be claimed from the eighth century for Fordwich downstream from Canterbury on the Stour. Again we do not know when either port was founded and modern archaeological investigation has not yet been undertaken.

Outside Kent, two large port settlements founded in the seventh or eighth centuries have been extensively excavated at Southampton and Ipswich. *Hamwic* (**colour plate 7**) was centred around St Mary's church to the east of the present centre of Southampton. Archaeology can show its existence by the early eighth century and also its gradual abandonment during the ninth. Ships will have been beached for loading and unloading on the west bank of the Itchen, where they could be refloated easily thanks to the double tides of the Solent.

The settlement covered 45ha (112 acres), of which some 3 per cent has been excavated, between 1946 and 1986. As no sites in the waterfront area of the port have become available to archaeologists, excavation has been concentrated on the zones in which manufacturing was taking place. A variety of crafts were practised using metals, bone, antler and possibly also glass. This settlement was laid out in a fairly regular manner, divided into plots by a rectilinear pattern of gravelled roads. The inland limits of the settlement were marked by a boundary ditch. Within the land plots were houses and workshops, wells and rubbish pits.

The contents of these pits tell us a great deal about the date range of the settlement from the types of objects being acquired and also made

there, as well as the organization which provided an adequate food-supply for an estimated population of 5000 or more. Cattle and sheep were brought in on the hoof, whereas pork may have arrived already butchered and salted in barrels. Not all the imported pottery, which came principally from northern France, need have been brought in as trade goods. There is the possibility that complete sets of French pottery accompanied Frankish merchants for their own personal use, but were left behind when they returned home on the completion of their business. It is usually seen as a West Saxon foundation within a royal estate called *Hamtun* and has been plausibly attributed to King Ine, whose name is also attached to a famous law code.

Ipswich or *Gipeswic* in Suffolk has its origins rather earlier, in the first half of the seventh century. Frankish wheelthrown pottery came principally from the Rhineland region nearby and only a small proportion arrived from northern France. There is also at least one probable Frankish burial in the recently excavated seventh- to eighth-century cemetery at Buttermarket here. Ipswich developed as a major pottery manufacturing centre from the eighth century, with a series of excavated kilns in which 'Ipswich Ware' was fired. As at *Hamwic*, there was some evidence for a rectilinear pattern of gravelled roads, and rubbish pits provide most of the archaeological finds. If Ipswich was also a royal foundation, then its location some 16km (10 miles) south of the Sutton Hoo barrows might be significant. Of course, as we have seen, Sutton Hoo need not be a royal burial ground. A rather smaller potential *wic* settlement may also have existed on the north side of the river Wensum in Norwich within the northern half of the East Anglian kingdom. A recent excavation there produced around 150 sherds of Ipswich Ware and imported Frankish pottery, but it may be some time before further opportunities for investigation occur here.

None of these sites had a direct Roman predecessor, though *Hamwic* lay downstream and on the opposite bank from a Roman walled settlement at Bitterne (*Clausentum*) and the town of *Venta Icenorum* is only a short distance to the south of Norwich. When Bede described London as an *emporium* to which merchants came from many lands, he was probably describing the London of his own day, rather than as it was at the very beginning of the seventh century. The vain search for this later seventh-to ninth-century trading settlement of *Lundenwic* within the walled Roman city has finally been abandoned. We now realize that it occupied open land a little upstream, centred on the Aldwych, the 'old *wic*' by the Strand, a beach on which ships could be drawn up. Recent excavations in Covent Garden and around Trafalgar Square have confirmed the results of a thorough survey of old discoveries. Between the seventh and ninth centuries the walled Roman town of *Lundenburh* may have been limited in its functions to an ecclesiastical centre around St Paul's cathedral and nearby royal residences in the north-west corner of the city.

There may have been a similar situation at York where an extensive seventh- to eighth-century settlement has been excavated at Fishergate, well away from the Roman fort and town. While the Fishergate site itself need not represent the trading centre of *Eoforwic*, the absence of Anglian settlement evidence from the Roman town and fort is no longer a cause for concern. The site of the cathedral occupies the centre of the Roman fort and Roman York seems likely to have had a limited role as an ecclesiastical and royal centre. Unfortunately the search for archaeological evidence to justify an equivalent trading settlement adjacent to Roman Lincoln at Wigford has failed, but we can expect to locate a few more *wic* sites in the future.

There is still a debate as to whether these manufacturing and trading centres founded in the seventh or eighth centuries should be regarded as towns. Certainly coins were being minted at London from the seventh century and at *Hamwic* during the eighth century. This,

and a relatively regular street layout at both Ipswich and *Hamwic*, suggest that they possessed some of the attributes of urban settlements. They are usually seen as royal foundations created to provide a secure and controllable market place on the margins of a kingdom. Kings could invite merchants from overseas to visit them without the risk of introducing too many foreign ideas to their subjects. A ruler might also expect the right of first refusal on luxury items, such as silk cloth. By controlling who entered and who left his port, the king could also decide who received the most desirable goods.

It would seem that from the seventh century onwards, each of the larger Anglo-Saxon kingdoms negotiated its own independent trade agreement with the Frankish kings. Their ports were matched by those of Rouen on the Seine, Quentovic on the Canche, Domburg on the Dutch coast and Dorestad on the Lower Rhine. These new arrangements would have replaced the monopoly apparently operated by the Franks through Kent in the sixth and early seventh centuries. As a result Kentish power, wealth and influence suffered a gradual decline through the seventh and eighth centuries.

Smaller market centres for the redistribution of goods brought into the major ports have proved much harder to identify. They need not even involve timber buildings, as they might well have had the character of an annual country fair. A site adjacent to an eighth-century coin hoard containing silver pennies of King Beonna at Middle Harling in north-west Suffolk might be one such centre. Another occurs near Ipswich at Barham, which has produced more finds of seventh- to eighth-century sceatta silver coins than Ipswich itself.

10
Late Anglo-Saxon England

The surviving records of the survey ordered by William I of the kingdom he had conquered, the *Domesday Book*, provide us with a detailed picture of most of England in 1066 and 1085. From it, for the first time, we can estimate the size of the population, at around 2 million. Perhaps one-tenth of those people now lived in towns, in stark contrast to the situation at the beginning of the seventh century, when there appear to be no towns as such. The majority still lived in the rural landscape with 13,418 named vills and 268,984 recorded individuals. Many of these vills now contained larger settlements organized as true villages, though in some parts of the country dispersed farms and small hamlets of similar size to those found in the Early Anglo-Saxon period continued to exist.

Open fields and nucleated villages
Anglo-Saxon England in the middle decades of the eleventh century possessed most of the characteristics associated with later medieval England under Norman, Angevin and Plantagenet rule. Open field agriculture with two or more common fields divided into narrow strips and crop rotation between the fields was well established across the Midlands and elsewhere. Tenth-century charter boundaries sometimes refer to headlands and other field features which are characteristic of open fields. Parts of such fields have also been discovered by archaeological excavation, preserved under the Norman castle mounds or mottes at Hen Domen (Montgomeryshire) and also at Sandal Castle (Yorkshire).

The nucleated village went hand in hand with the development of these field systems. Farming needed to become a co-operative effort when exploiting heavy clay soils with ox-drawn ploughs. As no one peasant farmer was likely to own enough oxen for a full plough team, the peasants would have to share, ploughing each others' strips in turn. The length of each strip was a furrow's length or furlong. This was the distance oxen could pull the plough before they needed to be rested and turned round to plough the next furrow.

There has been much debate as to when this field type was developed. The written sources are of little help here, as boundary clauses in charters before the ninth century do not give the sort of detailed information provided for tenth-century and later boundaries. Fortunately, in Northamptonshire, as in some other parts of the country, the ridge and furrow patterns of the medieval and later open fields can still be seen beneath the modern fields and have been mapped. On occasion we can compare this mapped record to estate maps of the seventeenth and eighteenth centuries showing the open fields before they were enclosed by acts of parliament. These accompany written surveys, which list who holds each strip or package of land on the estate.

Earlier estate surveys do not contain maps, but do list in turn each strip with its tenant's name. We can now map this information. The accumulated record can sometimes be taken back to the twelfth or thirteenth century. That is more or less as far as we can go, however, for a tenth- or eleventh-century charter for the estate will not list the component elements of its fields, as do the later surveys. At most, it will suggest that the ancestral version of the twelfth- and thirteenth-century fields were in existence within a century or so before the Norman Conquest.

Archaeological fieldwalking in Northamptonshire has recovered large concentrations of pottery associated with Late Anglo-Saxon settlements which seem to be of village size. These contrast with smaller accumulations of Middle Saxon pottery on other sites, which seem to imply hamlet-sized settlements of a similar scale to those of the Early period. As the change from hamlets and single farms to nucleated villages is intimately linked to the development of open fields, the date of the changeover from Middle Saxon pottery types to the Late Saxon forms becomes a matter of some importance. It seems to occur within the ninth century, but it is difficult to be very precise.

When searching for an explanation for the introduction and development of open fields, we have to be aware that the same process seems to be taking place over much of western Europe, including Denmark, around the same period. It seems to represent the last stage in a long process with origins in the Iron Age, which continued through the Roman period and beyond. Light loamy soils worked with ards, which had been favoured since the Neolithic and the Bronze Age, were becoming exhausted. It may be that the short-lived seventh-century settlement on Church Down, Chalton was based on a final attempt to plough the Roman and pre-Roman field systems of the South Downs. Over the centuries more and more of the population was forced to turn to ploughing heavier soils, which were very productive, but much harder to work. Gradually field shapes were modified to suit the true plough rather than the light ard.

After the seventh century, settlements on the South Downs are found in their dry valleys rather than on hilltops and increasingly the Downs came to be exploited as sheep pasture rather than for agriculture. Villages with Old English place-names on the spring line at the foot of the scarp of the Sussex Downs may well have been founded in the seventh or eighth centuries to exploit the productive soils on the south edge of the Weald. Other Anglo-Saxon farmers may have moved down on to the brickearth soils of the coastal plain to the south of the Downs around this period. Exploitation of the coastal region's soils goes back to the Iron Age and Roman period and the same was true of regions with heavy clay soils in East Anglia. Soil exhaustion of the older agricultural landscape will have combined with population pressures to a series of settlement shifts, as more communities turned to farming the heavier soils they had previously avoided.

Nevertheless, the nucleation of settlement and the creation of open fields in the Late Anglo-Saxon period may have been enforced as acts of lordship. Certainly the sizes of the estates being granted in tenth-century charters are markedly smaller than those being given in the eighth century. It seems probable that their recipients sought to compensate for this and maximize their income from the peasant farmers. In other words, they reorganized their fields and working methods to make them more productive. If this is correct, it clearly says something about the economic dependence and political subjection of peasant farmers on the owners of estates in the ninth century since their lords were able to get away with it.

Of course it is possible that there was some element of mutual advantage, in that the peasants may have been able to feed their families rather better under the new system. On the other hand, there may have been a loss of independence for the individual farmer and his family. Formerly they had worked the family's separate fields in return for a rent in the form of food or service renders to the lord of the estate. Now they had to exchange these for a number of dispersed strips within two or more great fields, farmed communally with their neighbours.

Parish and minister churches

Churches constructed by a lord to serve the spiritual needs of those working on an estate are a feature of the manorial entries in the Domesday Survey. Estate village churches often developed into parish churches and seem to emerge between the tenth and twelfth centuries. This helps to explain an often close match between the extents of later ecclesiastical parishes and Anglo-Saxon estate boundaries recorded in writing within the tenth and eleventh centuries. Prior to this period, parochial services were provided by a relatively small number of minster churches, mostly founded in the seventh and eighth centuries. Minster is the English term for a monastery and it seems that Anglo-Saxon monastic communities often included priests with duties to travel around very extensive 'parishes' serving the rural population.

The development of estate-sized parishes with a single priest to provide baptisms, the mass and burial in a graveyard adjacent to the church should be linked to the development of manorial organization based on nucleated villages and open fields. Loss of income to the minster churches from the diversion of fees for baptism and burial to the estate village church was countered by negotiating payments from the newly founded churches to the 'mother' minster church. It is by following the subsequent documentation of these payments between churches that it has proved possible to reconstruct much of the early minster church system.

Archaeological investigation of Anglo-Saxon stone churches, formerly the preserve of architectural historians, is becoming much more common. This is no longer limited to the excavation of the interior, which usually reveals a sequence of burials, pits for casting bells and the foundations of earlier building phases, occasionally including timber churches. Excavation outside in the graveyard can also be valuable, but great emphasis is now placed on combining such work with the investigation of the standing stone walls. If opportunities arise to strip off the plaster in the interior, or any modern rendering over the outer walls, a detailed analysis of the origins of the stone employed can tell us whether that stone was reused together with Roman brick from old Roman buildings or had been freshly quarried. Changes in the mortar used to bond the stonework imply separate construction phases. Combined with radiocarbon dates taken from fragments of wooden scaffolding in the walls, or from other materials used, this information can provide us with a detailed picture of the sequence of building. The long-term investigation of the church at Brixworth (Northamptonshire) is a good example, but others include churches at Barton-on-Humber (South Humberside), Repton (Derbyshire), Deerhurst (Gloucestershire) (85), Hadstock (Essex) and Rivenhall (Essex).

Monasteries
The recognition of large circular mortar mixers, in which great wooden paddles were pulled

85 *The north wall of the main rectangular church at Deerhurst (Glos.) stripped of plaster revealing details of its Anglo-Saxon stone construction.*

through the mortar around a central axis, illustrates the contribution of archaeology in enlarging our knowledge of Anglo-Saxon technology. These are known, for example, on a site next to St Peter's church at Northampton and at the monastery of Monkwearmouth in Sunderland. Surprisingly we know relatively little from excavation about the appearance of Anglo-Saxon monasteries. It seems that it was not until the tenth-century reforms of English monasteries associated with Dunstan, Oswald and Æthelwold and influenced by continental practice, that what we think of as the standard layout of medieval Benedictine monasteries was adopted here. Excavated evidence for a cloister, perhaps forming part of the infirmary of the New Minster at Winchester has yet to be fully published. There also seems to have been a cloister at St Augustine's Abbey, outside the walls of Canterbury, but as this was not excavated to modern standards it is not possible to be certain.

Much more can be said about the twin monasteries founded in the later seventh century by Benedict Biscop and abandoned in the ninth century at Monkwearmouth and Jarrow (**colour plate 8**). The final publication of the excavations at both sites will reveal clearly though that there was no fixed layout for monastic buildings in relation to their church or churches in Northumbria. Small rectangular timber buildings, which would not look out of place in a seventh- or eighth-century rural settlement have been excavated recently at Hartlepool. They might well represent the individual cells of monks or nuns at the documented double monastery of the seventh to ninth centuries there (**86**).

If so, it may be that other recently excavated Middle Saxon settlements of timber buildings were also monasteries. The site at Brandon (Suffolk) is one example, with a rectangular timber building which may have been a church, in view of the cemetery which surrounds it. Another such settlement was discovered even more recently at Flixborough near Scunthorpe (South Humberside). Finds of bronze stylus implements, which could be used to write on wax tablets, imply literacy and therefore monasticism on such sites. Clearly, we still have a great deal to learn from archaeology about the character and changing nature of monastic communities between the seventh and eleventh centuries.

86 *View of the foundation trenches of two buildings, possibly monastic cells, recently excavated at Hartlepool (Cleveland).*

Manors and thegns

As well as playing a leading role in founding churches on his (or her) estates, a Late Saxon lord (or lady) usually possessed a personal residence on the estate or manor. In some cases at least these residences were defended. For example, there is a substantial palisaded rampart and ditch enclosing a Late Saxon timber hall and other buildings at Goltho, on clay land to the north-east of Lincoln. This manorial centre was replaced after the Conquest by a Norman castle, whose construction removed evidence for some of the earlier buildings there. Other Late Saxon manor houses which had defences, or at the very least were enclosed by a bank and ditch, are known from excavations at Sulgrave (Northamptonshire), Faccombe Netherton (Hampshire) and Portchester Castle (Hampshire) (**colour plate 9**). All of these were the precursors of later Norman manor houses or castles.

A Late Anglo-Saxon text lists the property qualifications that might permit a successful farmer or ceorl to be recognized by the king as a lord or thegn:

> and if a ceorl prospered, that he possessed fully five hides of land of his own, a bell and a burh-gate, a seat and special office in the king's hall, then he was henceforth entitled to the rights of a thegn.

Unfortunately this description receives no confirmation in any of the surviving Anglo-Saxon law codes, so we cannot assess its validity. The bell referred to might well have been hung in a tower. If the substantial stone building whose foundations were excavated at Portchester Castle was not a small chapel, it might have been such a tower. Old English *burh* can simply mean a fortified place, though over time it came to be applied particularly to a defended town and is the origin for the word borough. It is unfortunate that the Norman castle earthworks at Goltho disturbed the one area where there might have been a fortified gateway. As a result, we still do not have much idea of what form such a gate building might have taken.

Nevertheless, at Goltho we seem to be very

close to the modern historian's definition of a medieval castle as the defended residence of a lord and his household. The Normans certainly introduced the newest form of continental private fortifications to England after 1066 and a few castles may have been constructed a little earlier by Normans in the service of Edward the Confessor. Yet the Norman constructions in earth and timber of a ringwork, with or without a tower on a mound or motte, may not have seemed particularly strange to the Anglo-Saxon peasants who were press-ganged into the labouring work.

The absence of fortification is a feature of earlier estate centres in the seventh and eighth centuries, as we have seen at Cowdery's Down and Yeavering. Admittedly there is the great palisaded enclosure on the east side of Yeavering, but this has no ditch outside it. As an external ditch is an invaluable component of any serious defence against a military force, it seems more probable that this enclosure was primarily intended to protect livestock from predatory animals and cattle raiders.

This is not to claim that the Anglo-Saxons made no use of forts between the fifth and seventh centuries. There were former British coastal promontory forts, such as Bamburgh (Northumberland), which Bede and other written sources reveal was used by Bernician kings as a stronghold. Doubtless other hillforts as well as walled Roman towns and forts could be easily adapted as defensible refuges in the event of a surprise attack. On the other hand, most rural settlements could be sacrificed and abandoned to be ransacked and burnt down as at Yeavering. After all, providing timber was in plentiful supply, they could be rebuilt easily enough. There was not a lot of point in fortifying such places, when their individual buildings had a limited life and had to be replaced at regular intervals.

It seems probable that the Viking raids and campaigns of conquest in the later eighth and ninth centuries created a major change in attitudes to fortification. The trading settlements of *Hamwic* and London's *wic* along the Strand show no sign of defences. The same is true of the port at Dorestad on the Lower Rhine. These settlements proved to be too large and prosperous to be lightly abandoned when attacked by Viking sea raiders. Instead, most mercantile sites were gradually depopulated during the ninth century as their occupants sought the shelter of strong walls fronted by ditches to keep out Scandinavian armies.

Burhs and urban development

The population of London moved back from *Lundenwic* into the walled city of *Lundenburh*. This had been largely deserted since the Roman period, apart from the cathedral of St Paul's, founded in the seventh century and a few royal residences nearby in the Cripplegate area. Perhaps part of the population of *Hamwic* settled behind the Roman stone walls at Bitterne (*Clausentum*), a little way upstream to the north on the river Itchen in the ninth century. In any case, at some stage in the Late Saxon period a fortified town was founded on a fresh site to the west of *Hamwic*, by the river Test, which was to develop into the later medieval town of Southampton.

The first organized construction programme of public defences for major settlements may have been achieved by the Mercian kingdom in the eighth to ninth centuries. This would be appropriate, in view of the tradition that the series of massive banks, each fronted by a ditch, along the Welsh Marches was constructed at the command of the Mercian king Offa in the eighth century (**87**). Surveys and research excavations which are still in progress on Offa's Dyke indicate that the history of its construction is complex and, as finds are virtually absent from its banks and ditches, very difficult to date. It remains a remarkable achievement of civil organization, as the identification of lengths built by individual workgangs confirms. A sector seems to have been assigned separately to each community which owed obligations to perform labour services for the king.

Duties of estate owners to contribute labour and materials to the building of fortifications and bridges are first specifically mentioned in eighth-century Mercian charters. Bridges were particularly important in helping to deny enemy ships easy access inland by river. Evidence at Hereford for an early defensive bank and ditch cannot be dated directly, but does precede early tenth-century Anglo-Saxon defences there. They may perhaps represent late eighth- or ninth-century Mercian defences for a planned town there.

If this is correct, then the programme of building *burhs* (forts and fortified towns) associated with Alfred in the late ninth century

to defend the West Saxon kingdom from the Vikings seems likely to have borrowed from Mercian experience. A document called the *Burghal Hidage* lists these *burhs* and also some of those built at the orders of his immediate successor Edward the Elder. This lists the number of land units (hides) attached to each *burh* in England south of the Thames (excluding Kent and London for reasons which are not entirely clear). It was the duty of the rural estates assigned to each *burh* to provide resources to ensure that its fortifications were properly maintained and that an adequate rotating garrison of part-time soldiers was available at all times to defend it.

87 An air view of a section of Offa's Dyke in Shropshire. (Cambridge University Collection: copyright reserved.)

88 Air photo of the town of Wallingford which still preserves elements of its defences and layout as a West Saxon burh *founded to combat the threat of Viking invasion in the later ninth century. (Cambridge University Collection: copyright reserved.)*

Alfred's *burhs* included former Roman towns, like Winchester, whose stone walls were repaired and to which a pair of ditches seems to have been added. There were also some short-lived forts which were clearly too small to develop into towns, for instance the earthwork enclosure at Burpham near Arundel (West Sussex). They also include substantial new towns set out on relatively flat land with a square or rectangular layout, as at Oxford, Wallingford (88), Cricklade (Oxfordshire) and Wareham (Dorset). These were based on two gravelled main streets meeting at a central crossroads, which could act as market places. An intramural or wall street, running parallel to and behind ramparts, is another important feature, found in both the redeveloped former Roman towns and these new foundations. This will have allowed the garrison to move rapidly and unseen from one section of the defences to another. Lastly there were new towns founded on naturally defensible sites, such as spurs of high ground or promontories as at Lewes (East Sussex) and Lydford (Devon). These frequently have a more restricted plan and street layout.

In the first half of the tenth century, Edward and his successors made the construction and garrisoning of this type of fortified site a key element in their systematic conquest of eastern and northern England. This enabled them to seize and maintain control of the Danelaw settled by Scandinavian armies in the ninth century. The creation of a unified kingdom of

England was the end result and, although this kingdom was to be seized by the Danish king Cnut at the beginning of the eleventh century, it was later restored to a descendant of Edward the Elder we know as Edward the Confessor.

The contribution of the Vikings was not limited to stimulating the development of fortified centres in England, for flourishing trade and manufacture is a feature of the towns which developed in the regions controlled by the Scandinavians. Excavated sites at Coppergate in York and Flaxengate in Lincoln have provided us with a wealth of evidence for industrial and commercial activity. The systematic provision of fortified towns not only provided places of refuge for the Anglo-Saxon rural population within a 24km (15 mile) radius in the event of Viking attack, they provided a framework of secure regional market centres throughout the English kingdom.

Coinage and the evidence for mints perhaps provides one of the best guides to the relative prosperity of individual towns. Anglo-Saxon kings exercised a strict control over the issue of coins in the tenth and eleventh centuries

89 *Part of a hoard of Edward the Confessor pennies (Helmet type) from Springthorpe (Lincolnshire).*

(89). From *c*.973 onwards, the whole coinage was reminted every six or seven years by moneyers in sixty or more towns, all striking coins of the same design. This was a national coinage, with coins circulating rapidly around the entire English kingdom, as the composition of such coin hoards as that from Pemberton's Parlour in Chester, makes clear. This hoard was deposited around 979-80 and though the earliest coins in it were no more than six years old when buried, they came from mints which represent most regions of England.

The payment of taxes, fines and officially-witnessed commercial transactions could only be made in the current valid coinage. The majority of towns had no more than one moneyer, but larger centres would have a number of moneyers to meet the demand for silver coin. Ranking lists of mints can be produced by comparing the number of moneyers' names for each mint linked to each coin type. London was the most important mint of all in the tenth

and eleventh centuries followed by Lincoln or York, then Winchester; Chester, Thetford, Exeter or Stamford belong in the next rank down at different times.

A distinctive urban architecture based on timber buildings constructed over cellars dug into the subsoil built along gravelled street frontages makes its first appearance in these Late Anglo-Saxon towns. Waterlogged timbers from such buildings reused in revetments along the river frontage in London have enabled archaeologists to reconstruct their carpentry and appearance in some detail (90). The enlargement of towns is one measure of their success. For example, there is the evidence that Oxford was expanded eastwards from its almost square original layout to take in the entire area enclosed by its later medieval walls before the

90 *Reconstruction of a Late Anglo-Saxon timber building in London. (Drawing by Chrissie Milne; Museum of London.)*

Norman Conquest, including the church of St Peter in the East. Another is the not infrequent evidence of suburbs outside town gates by the time of the Domesday Survey.

A multiplicity of small parish churches seems to have been another characteristic of English towns by the eleventh century. Their foundation seems to represent the urban counterpart of the creation of rural parish churches on individual estates. It may also reflect the frequent attachment of blocks of town properties to rural estates, which provided their owners with direct access to the manufacturing centres and markets of the towns.

Royal palaces and hunting lodges

Royal palaces existed in some of the more important towns and it seems, for example, that Edward the Confessor spent a great deal of time at London, Gloucester and Winchester. Edward's role in refounding and redeveloping Westminster Abbey provided the basis for the development of Westminster as the premier royal centre under his Norman and Angevin successors. The dimensions of his royal hall at Westminster may be reconstructed from those of the surviving Norman stone hall, which was built around the still-standing timber structure.

A rural Late Saxon royal residence has been excavated at Cheddar to compare to the earlier, seventh-century complex at Yeavering. Cheddar appears in King Alfred's will as part of his personal property rather than as a royal centre as such, but it seems to have become a royal property in the tenth century. We know that the king's council (*witan*) met there on three occasions, in 941, 956 and 968, and it also functioned as a base for the traditional royal pursuit of hunting. The ninth-century residence is centred around a long timber hall. This was followed by a major reorganization of the site shortly after c.930 (**91**). A small stone chapel was constructed over the site of the earlier hall and a new timber hall which was both shorter and wider than its predecessor was built to the south. Both private chapel and hall were rebuilt at the end of the tenth century on the same sites. Although enclosed by a fence, this settlement cannot be convincingly described as being fortified. In this, as in other respects, Cheddar in

91 *Reconstruction of the royal hunting lodge at Cheddar in the tenth century. (Alan Sorrell; Illustrated London News.)*

the tenth and eleventh centuries is not very different from Yeavering. There is not sufficient permanent accommodation to house the entire royal court and we must suppose that much of the royal retinue camped in tents around the main buildings.

Conclusion

This brief sketch of the range of archaeological evidence brings out the clear differences between England in the early seventh century and the mid-eleventh century. Those differences particularly reflect two major influences for change. The first of these was the establishment of the Christian Church, which quickly became a major landowner in the seventh and eighth centuries. Clergymen proved highly influential in their attempts to guide the actions of kings. The Church brought with it literacy in Latin and Greek and provided close contact with those regions of western Europe in which a great part of the Roman legacy had been preserved. The second influence was the Viking raids and invasions between the eighth and eleventh centuries, which did so much to change and shape the character of eastern and northern England, as well as those of the Scottish Isles, the Isle of Man and Ireland.

We still have a great deal more to learn about the archaeology of England between the seventh and ninth centuries, or the Middle Saxon period as it is usually termed. The wealth of evidence available from the fully-dressed individuals of the Early Saxon cemeteries comes to an end in the early eighth century. There is something of a gap between their last burials and the first excavated graves with bodies wrapped in shrouds from Christian churchyard cemeteries, such as at Barton-on-Humber and Raunds (Northamptonshire).

Settlement shift seems likely to have accompanied the abandonment of the Early Saxon cemeteries and settlements in the seventh to eighth centuries, but the combination of field-work and excavation has yet to reveal an adequate sample of settlements for us to begin to be able to describe a complete settlement history. We await with particular interest the results of a long-term project based around Raunds, with excavations of settlements of the Early, Middle and Late Saxon periods. Equally important as the developments occurring between the seventh and eighth centuries is the clear need for us to achieve a better understanding of the transition from Middle to Late Saxon England in the ninth century. Major changes in the organization of settlements and the exploitation of the landscape took place around this time and archaeology can make a major contribution here.

Appendix

Once excavated, Early Anglo-Saxon burial and settlement sites do not provide much indication that there was anything there. You can park your car next to the Yeavering royal settlement and read the English Heritage plaque in front of an open grass field, but you will have to supply any reconstruction in your own imagination. The only site open to the public with reconstructed timber buildings of this period is at West Stow near Bury St Edmunds in Suffolk (with special booking arrangements for school parties). The excavation programme at Sutton Hoo near Woodbridge in Suffolk was completed in October 1991, but there should still be guided tours of the barrow mounds there in the early afternoon at weekends from Easter until late September over the next few years.

In many ways, museums provide rather better access to the archaeology of this period. While many county and local museums in England contain at least a small display of local Anglo-Saxon material from both cemeteries and settlements, the outstanding collections are to be found in the British Museum in London and the Ashmolean Museum in Oxford. Both of these contain representative material from most regions of Anglo-Saxon England. Any appreciation of the rich Kentish finds requires a visit to Liverpool City Museum to see Faussett's collection there, as well as to the Museum of the Kent Archaeological Society at Maidstone. The University Museum of Archaeology and Anthropology in Cambridge also has an important regional collection, as does Sheffield Museum, which contains many finds from barrow burials in the Peak District including the Benty Grange helmet. In Wiltshire the museums in Devizes and Salisbury are well worth a visit, as is the Yorkshire Museum in York.

By contrast the stone churches built from the seventh century onwards are highly visible monuments. For example a trip to Canterbury could include a visit to the English Heritage site of the monastery of St Augustine with the ruined walls of three Anglo-Saxon churches dedicated to St Peter and St Paul, St Mary, and St Pancras. A short walk up the hill immediately east brings the visitor to the still used parish church of St Martin. This may well have developed from a small private chapel used by Æthelberht's Frankish queen. Similarly in Tyne and Wear the still standing churches at Monkwearmouth and Jarrow provide a direct link to the monasteries of the seventh to ninth centuries there and to the Venerable Bede. There is a museum at Jarrow to illustrate the rich evidence acquired through the excavation of these two sites. The best guide to stone churches containing Anglo-Saxon constructional work remains H.M. & J. Taylor, *Anglo-Saxon Architecture* (3 vols. 1965 & 1978) while the reader may find a book such as L. & J. Laing, *A Guide to the Dark Age Remains in Britain* (1979) useful when attempting to locate stone churches, sculptures and other visible and upstanding monuments of the later Anglo-Saxon period.

Further reading

Chapter 1 (pp.9–13)

J. Campbell (ed.), *The Anglo-Saxons* (Phaidon 1982 & Penguin 1991) provides a general introduction to the Anglo-Saxons.

L. Webster, Anglo-Saxon England AD 400–1100, in *Archaeology in Britain since 1945*, eds. I. Longworth & J. Cherry (BMP, London 1986), pp.119–59 is a general survey of their archaeology.

J. N. L. Myres, 'The Angles, Saxons, and the Jutes', *Proceedings of the British Academy*, LVI, 1970, pp.145–74 summarizes the archaeology linking England to north Germany and south Scandinavia.

M. Gelling, *Signposts to the Past: Place-Names and the History of England* (Dent, London 1978) and *Place-names in the Landscape* (Dent, London 1984) provide an introduction to the place-name evidence.

E. Southworth, *Anglo-Saxon Cemeteries: A Reappraisal* (Stroud 1990) contains essays by S. C. Hawkes and M. Rhodes on Bryan Faussett and the early history of his collection.

Chapters 2–4 (pp.14–53)

The Chalton settlement has not yet been published, but interim reports can be found in *Medieval Archaeology*, XVI, 1972, pp.13–31 & XVII, 1973, 1–25 and *Current Archaeology*, 59, 1977, 364–9.

M. Millett and S. James, 'Excavations at Cowdery's Down, Basingstoke, Hampshire, 1978–81', *Archaeological Journal*, 140, 151–279.

S. James, A. Marshall and M. Millett, 'An Early Medieval Building Tradition', *Archaeological Journal*, 141, 182–215 considers the reconstruction of halls and debates their origins.

M. Bell, 'Excavations at Bishopstone: The Anglo-Saxon Period', *Sussex Archaeological Collections*, 115, 1977, pp.193–241.

S. West, *West Stow: The Anglo-Saxon Village*, East Anglian Archaeology 24 (Bury St Edmunds 1985).

H. Hamerow, *Excavations at Mucking. Volume 2: The Anglo-Saxon Settlement*, English Heritage Archaeological Report 21 (London 1991).

B. Cunliffe and T. Rowley (eds.), *Lowland Iron Age Communities in Europe*, BAR International Series 48 (Oxford 1978) contains essays by P. Schmid & W. H. Zimmerman in English on the settlements at Feddersen Wierde and Flögeln in N. Germany.

W. A. van Es, *Wijster: A Native Village beyond the Imperial Frontier 150–425 A.D.*, Palaeohistoria 11 (Groningen 1967)

E. T. Leeds published three reports on his Sutton Courtenay excavations, which appeared in *Archaeologia*, LXIII, 1923, pp.147–92; LXXVI, 1927, pp.59–80; XCII, 1947, pp.79–93.

M. L. Faull (ed.), *Studies in Late Anglo-Saxon Settlement* (Oxford 1984) contains papers by S. Losco-Bradley & H. M. Wheeler on Catholme and Dunston's Clump and by I. M. Smith analysing the Sprouston air photo evidence.

M. Gardiner, 'An Anglo-Saxon and Medieval Settlement at Botolphs, Bramber, West Sussex', *Archaeological Journal*, 147, 1990, pp.216–75.

B. Hope-Taylor, *Yeavering: An Anglo-British centre of early Northumbria*, DOE Archaeological Report 7 (HMSO London 1977).

L. Alcock, *Economy, Society and Warfare among the Britons and Saxons*, (University of Wales Press, Cardiff 1987) contains a discussion of the hierarchy of royal centres in Northumbria.

J. H. Williams, M. Shaw and V. Denham, *Middle Saxon Palaces at Northampton* (Northampton 1984).

P. Sawyer, 'The Royal *Tun* in Pre-Conquest England', in *Ideal and Reality in Frankish and Anglo-Saxon Society*, eds. P. Wormald, D. Bullough and R. Collins (Blackwell, Oxford 1983) pp.273–99 considers the written sources for royal centres in Anglo-Saxon England.

Chapters 5–7 (pp.54–96)

A. Meaney, *A Gazetteer of Anglo-Saxon Burial Sites* (Allen & Unwin, London 1964) provides an annotated list of Early Anglo-Saxon cemeteries reported prior to *c*.1960; more recent discoveries are listed in annual reports in *Medieval Archaeology*.

C. Hogarth, 'Structural features in Anglo-Saxon graves', *Archaeological Journal*, 130, 1976, pp.104–19.

N. Reynolds, 'The structure of Anglo-Saxon graves', *Antiquity*, 50, 1976, pp.140–4.

S. C. Hawkes, 'Sunrise dating of death and burial in an Anglo-Saxon cemetery in East Kent', *Archaeologia Cantiana*, 92, 1976, pp.33–51.

A series of articles on grave orientation in *Archaeological Journal*, 135, 1978, pp.1–14; 139, 1982, pp.101–23; and 140, 1983, pp.322–8.

P. Rahtz, T. Dickinson and L. Watts (eds.), *Anglo-Saxon Cemeteries 1979*, BAR British Series 82 (Oxford 1982).

L. Jørgensen, 'Family Burial Practices and Inheritance Systems. The Development of an Iron Age Society from 500 B.C to A.D. 1000 on Bornholm, Denmark', *Acta Archaeologica* 58, 1987, pp.17–53.

A. Boddington, A. N. Garland and R. C. Janaway (eds.) *Death, Decay and Reconstruction: Approaches to Archaeology and Forensic Science* (Manchester 1987).

C. A. Roberts, F. Lee and J. Bintliff (eds.), *Burial Archaeology: Current Research, Methods and Developments*, BAR British Series 211 (Oxford 1989) contains a number of useful papers by J. Henderson, J. McKinley and C. Hills.

G. R. Owen-Crocker, *Dress in Anglo-Saxon England* (Manchester University Press 1986).

J. D. Richards, *The Significance of Form and Decoration of Anglo-Saxon Cremation Urns*, BAR British Series 166 (Oxford 1987).

S. C. Hawkes (ed.), *Weapons and Warfare in Anglo-Saxon England*, Oxford University Committee for Archaeology 21 (Oxford 1989), especially H. Härke's paper.

S. Hirst, *An Anglo-Saxon Inhumation Cemetery at Sewerby, East Yorkshire*, York University Archaeological Publications 4 (York 1985).

V. I. Evison, *Dover: the Buckland Anglo-Saxon Cemetery*, English Heritage Archaeological Report 3 (London 1987).

A. Down and M. Welch, *Chichester Excavations 7: Apple Down & The Mardens* (Chichester 1990).

C. Hills *et al.* (eds.), *The Anglo-Saxon Cemetery at Spong Hill, North Elmham*, Parts I-IV, East Anglian Archaeology 6, 11, 21, 34 (Gressenhall 1977, 1981, 1984 & 1987).

B. Yorke, *Kings and Kingdoms of Early Anglo-Saxon England* (Seaby, London 1990) surveys the historical evidence in depth.

G. Speake, *A Saxon Bed Burial on Swallowcliffe Down*, English Heritage Archaeological Report 10 (London 1989).

R. Bruce-Mitford (ed.), *The Sutton Hoo Ship-Burial*, 3 volumes (BMP London 1975, 1978 & 1983).

R. Bruce-Mitford *Aspects of Anglo-Saxon Archaeology: Sutton Hoo and other discoveries* (Gollancz, London 1974) collects papers which discuss among other sites the finds from Snape, Taplow and Benty Grange.

Bulletin of the Sutton Hoo Research Committee 1, 1983–7, 1990 etc. contain annual reports on the research excavation of Sutton Hoo.

Chapter 8 (pp.97–107)

J. N. L. Myres and B. Green, *The Anglo-Saxon Cemeteries of Caistor-by-Norwich and Markshall, Norfolk*, Society of Antiquaries of London Research Report 30 (London 1973).

W. I. Roberts, *Romano-Saxon Pottery*, BAR British Series 106 (Oxford 1982).

V. A. Maxfield (ed.), *The Saxon Shore: A Handbook*, Exeter Studies in History 25 (Exeter 1989) especially the paper by S. C. Hawkes.

G. Clarke, *The Roman Cemetery at Lankhills*, Winchester Studies 3, Pre-Roman and Roman Winchester, Part II (OUP, Oxford 1979).

S. E. Cleary, *The Ending of Roman Britain* (Batsford, London 1989).

Chapter 9 (pp.108–119)

W. A. Oddy (ed.) *Aspects of Early Metallurgy*, British Museum Occasional Paper 17 (London 1980), especially the papers by K. Lamm on Helgö and M. U. Jones on Mucking.

L. Webster (ed.) *Aspects of Production and Style in Dark Age Metalwork*, British Museum Occasional Paper 34 (London 1982).

J. W. Huggett, 'Imported Grave Goods and the Early Anglo-Saxon Economy', *Medieval Archaeology*, 32, 1988, pp.63–96.

C. Scull, 'Scales and weights in Early Anglo-Saxon England', *Archaeological Journal*, 147, 1990, pp.183–215.

R. Hodges and B. Hobley (eds.), *The Rebirth of Towns in the West AD 700-1050*, CBA Research Report 68 (London 1988).

Chapter 10 (pp.120–132)

D. M. Wilson (ed.), *The Archaeology of Anglo-Saxon England* (Methuen, London 1976; CUP Paperback, Cambridge 1986) provides an introduction to the archaeology of the seventh to eleventh centuries.

D. Hooke (ed.), *Anglo-Saxon Settlements* (Blackwell, Oxford 1988).

R. Morris, *Churches in the Landscape* (Dent, London 1989).

W. Rodwell, *English Heritage Book of Church Archaeology* (Batsford, London 1989).

R. Daniels, 'The Anglo-Saxon Monastery at Church Close', *Archaeological Journal*, 145, 1988, pp.158–210.

R. D. Carr, A. Tester and P. Murphy, 'The Middle-Saxon Settlement at Staunch Meadow, Brandon', *Antiquity* 62, 1988, pp.371–7.

G. Beresford, *Goltho: the development of an early medieval manor c.850-1150*, English Heritage Archaeological Report 4 (London 1987).

J. R. Fairbrother, *Faccombe Netherton: Excavations of a Saxon and Medieval Manorial Complex*, British Museum Occasional Paper 74 (London 1990).

P. Rahtz, *The Saxon and Medieval Palaces at Cheddar*, BAR British Series 65 (Oxford 1979).

M. Carver, *Underneath English Towns: Interpreting Urban Archaeology* (Batsford, London 1987)

A. Vince, *Saxon London: An Archaeological Investigation* (Seaby, London 1990).

Glossary

annular adjective meaning ring-shaped, commonly used in the description of a ring-shaped brooch (annular brooch) or a ring-shaped ditch (annular ditch) and contrasts with an incomplete or penannular ring.

ard a primitive form of scratch plough pulled by livestock, usually a pair of oxen, and developed from a hoe, which creates a shallow furrow without turning over the soil. The Anglo-Saxons used both the ard and the true plough with a mould-board to turn over the soil.

barrow from Old English *beorg* meaning a burial mound. The Anglo-Saxons reused standing prehistoric barrows for burial, but also constructed their own round barrows. Another Old English word for a barrow was *hlæw*.

Benedictine the principal monastic regulations to be adopted widely in western Europe were those first established in Italy by St Benedict.

bracteate a sheet metal disc-shaped pendant ornament, usually of gold, decorated with *repoussé* designs. Introduced to England from south Scandinavia in the later fifth century.

brooch the principal dress fastener in Early Anglo-Saxon female costume up to the seventh century – types mentioned are *cruciform* brooches with a cross pattern formed by the knobs on the top and sides of the headplate; *equal-arm* brooches with two triangular plates either side of a short linking bow; *saucer* brooches with a shallow rim on a disc a bit like a tea saucer; *square-headed* brooches with a rectangular headplate; and *supporting-arm* brooches with a long bar which supports the spring mechanism of the pin; additionally in the fourth and fifth centuries Roman army officers wore *crossbow* brooches on their cloaks, whose upper bar has an 'onion-shaped' knob at each end.

Brytenwealda and ***Bretwalda*** are two versions of a title given in different copies of the *Anglo-Saxon Chronicle* which can be translated respectively as 'wide-ruler' and 'ruler of Britain'. Bede does not provide an equivalent title in Latin for such overlord kings, but describes them as exercising *imperium* (rule) over other kings south of the Humber.

burh a fortified place, either a fort or in the Late Anglo-Saxon period more often a defended town, which usage leads to the word borough.

cabochon a precious or semi-precious gemstone which is only polished and not cut into facets before being set into jewellery.

chamber grave an unusually large and deep timber-lined grave, which formed a room-sized chamber in which a wide range of objects could be deposited in addition to the corpse.

civitas the origin of our word city, a Roman *civitas* was an administrative district centred on a town. While an Anglo-Saxon *civitas* was an important and probably fortified royal centre, it was not necessarily a former Roman town for the term could be used to describe a promontory fort or hillfort such as Bamburgh (Northumberland).

clamp-kiln the simplest form of kiln for firing

pottery, consisting of a bonfire covering a cluster of clay pots.

co-axial fields or fields on a common axis, is the preferred term for an early type of field, which is relatively small and usually square or rectangular in shape and associated with the cross-ploughing technique of the ard plough. They are often referred to as Celtic fields, but their origins are now known to go back to the Late Neolithic and Early Bronze Age, making this an inappropriate term.

cremation burning a corpse on or under a pyre (bonfire).

cruck stout inward-curved timbers called crucks are normally used in matched pairs fastened together with one or more horizontal timbers to provide a secure load-bearing support for the roof of a building.

girdle hangers established term for pairs of symbolic non-functional keys found in female graves of the fifth and sixth centuries.

Grubenhaus/Grubenhäuser standard German term for a timber building based on a man-made hollow, literally a 'pit house', see also under *sunken featured building* (SFB).

hall standard term applied to any rectangular timber building with a floor at ground level or above in an Anglo-Saxon settlement, typically with a pair of door openings in the middle of the long side. Hall-house is the term used by German archaeologists to describe a continental building form which combines a rectangular living area with a byre containing stalls for animals, chiefly cattle.

hide a taxable land unit, the equivalent of Bede's *familia* and notionally sufficient to support an extended family. A hide cannot be expressed in terms of so many acres or hectares, as its size would vary according to the productivity of the land. Hidage is a land valuation for the purposes of levying either a tax or military and related labour services, e.g. the *Tribal Hidage* and the *Burghal Hidage*.

inhumation placing a corpse in the earth i.e. a grave.

lathe traditional term used in Kent for a large administrative district within that county. The equivalent districts in Sussex are called rapes.

loomweights rings of fired clay used as weights on a vertical loom, being attached to the bottom of the warp threads to provide tension.

mausoleum a tomb usually of stone and/or brick construction.

minster English word for a monastery. A minster church is a former Anglo-Saxon monastery which originally sent priests on circuit to provide pastoral care for a large *parochia* before the creation of churches for the much smaller parishes with which we are familiar today.

model either in cast metal techniques a former around which a clay mould was made, or in *repoussé* decorated sheet metalwork an ornamented die which can be pressed, rubbed or hammered against the metal foil.

non-metrical traits characteristics which can be described, but not measured, as applied to the study of human and animal skeletons.

peplos an item of female costume consisting of a long tube of cloth worn as a dress fastened at the neck.

pottery ornament pottery can be decorated in a variety of ways before it is fired, e.g. pushing out part of the side wall and/or adding clay externally to form a protruding boss; incising lines with a tool in a variety of patterns, such as a rising curve or *standing arch*, a freehand drawing of an animal, runes etc.; and using antler stamps to apply an animal design, runic characters or a geometric pattern etc.

prone burial with the corpse placed face-down.

radiocarbon dating a method of dating organic materials up to 70,000 years old by measuring the radioactive carbon isotope carbon 14 (C14), which decays at a known rate following death. In practice the C14 decay rate can be checked against tree rings on both living and ancient trees giving corrected (i.e. calibrated) dates for a more accurate result.

Dates are expressed as a central year ± a standard deviation, which represents only a 66 per cent certainty that the date of death of the tree etc. lies within the range quoted. The degree of accuracy can be increased only by doubling or tripling the standard deviation.

repoussé technique of working sheet metal by pressing, rubbing or hammering a die on to a thin metal foil. The French term refers to the design being applied from the back and the decorative pattern standing out in relief on the front of the foil.

runes/runic alphabet characters and an alphabet originally designed for incision in wood with long vertical strokes cut across the grain and short slanting strokes, originating in south Scandinavia around the first century AD and introduced to Britain by the Anglo-Saxons.

shingle a wooden roof tile.

sunken featured building abbreviated as SFB, has become the standard English term for a *Grubenhaus*.

supine burial with the corpse placed extended on its back.

Terp standard Dutch term for a man-made mound constructed for a settlement in a coastal location exposed to periodic flooding. *Wierde* and *Wurt* are equivalent German terms.

thermoluminescence dating a method of dating pottery and other fired clay items by measuring the amount of energy released as light when heated above a crucial temperature. Thermoluminescence (TL) is created by ionizing radiation in the crystal lattice over the time since the clay was last heated to that temperature. It usually measures the time lapse since the kiln firing of a pot. With burnt daub from a building destroyed by fire, it should provide the date of that fire. Dates are expressed with a standard deviation, see *radiocarbon dating*.

unurned cremation a deposit of burnt bone which is not found in a identifiable container or urn.

vill territorial unit corresponding to a modern township or civil parish.

villa the country residence of a Roman noble based on a working farm and owned in combination with a residence in a town, the same term was used by Bede to describe an Anglo-Saxon royal estate centre as an alternative to *vicus* or a Roman rural settlement or farm.

wall plate the timbers which mark the top of a timber wall in a roofed building.

wic an Anglo-Saxon trading port and manufacturing centre characteristically had a name ending in this Old English place-name element, which seems to be derived from Latin *vicus* meaning a rural settlement or farm, e.g. *Lundenwic*. Place-names in *wic* were also used to mean a saltworks, a street, or a dwelling and dependent farm.

Wierde see *Terp*.

wrist clasps eye and catch fittings sewn (or rivetted) in pairs on to the split ends of the long sleeves belonging to an Anglian female undergarment, which clasped the sleeve cuff together when fastened.

Wurt see *Terp*.

Index

(Page numbers in **bold** refer to illustrations)